To Dear Davis —

May you continue to
Shine Bright ...

Best Wishes

Nirmu 😊

Discover Your TRUE Self and Live Your BEST Life TODAY!

Introducing a NEW Concept for Living Life on Earth

*A path
to a more happier, peaceful, rewarding and meaningful life
on earth at this present time*

Niroma De Zoysa

BALBOA
PRESS
A DIVISION OF HAY HOUSE

Copyright © 2018 Niroma De Zoysa.

All rights reserved. No part of this book may be used or reproduced by any means, graphic, electronic, or mechanical, including photocopying, recording, taping or by any information storage retrieval system without the written permission of the author except in the case of brief quotations embodied in critical articles and reviews.

Balboa Press books may be ordered through booksellers or by contacting:

Balboa Press
A Division of Hay House
1663 Liberty Drive
Bloomington, IN 47403
www.balboapress.com
1 (877) 407-4847

Because of the dynamic nature of the Internet, any web addresses or links contained in this book may have changed since publication and may no longer be valid. The views expressed in this work are solely those of the author and do not necessarily reflect the views of the publisher, and the publisher hereby disclaims any responsibility for them.

The author of this book does not dispense medical advice or prescribe the use of any technique as a form of treatment for physical, emotional, or medical problems without the advice of a physician, either directly or indirectly. The intent of the author is only to offer information of a general nature to help you in your quest for emotional and spiritual well-being. In the event you use any of the information in this book for yourself, which is your constitutional right, the author and the publisher assume no responsibility for your actions.

Any people depicted in stock imagery provided by Getty Images are models, and such images are being used for illustrative purposes only. Certain stock imagery © Getty Images.

Print information available on the last page.

ISBN: 978-1-9822-1434-0 (sc)
ISBN: 978-1-9822-1432-6 (hc)
ISBN: 978-1-9822-1433-3 (e)

Library of Congress Control Number: 2018912524

Balboa Press rev. date: 11/08/2018

To Boo . . .

My Beloved
The one I love
and the one who loves me unconditionally

Contents

Phase One 1
Phase Two 41
Phase Three 63
Conclusion 77

First and foremost, I am deeply grateful my Source has chosen me to write this book. I don't know why he chose me because there are many talented and renowned writers of this world who could do this – better than me. However, I am blessed to have received this opportunity and it is my hope I am able to a good job. Thank you, dear Source for the opportunity.

This book is written based on the wisdom I received from my Source/Creator. I call my Source/Creator "God" - but please note, this is not about a religion. I do not belong to any religion at this present time and I also do not know enough about any religion. I respect all religions. I am instructed to write this book NOW and present it to people who are OPEN to receiving this information at this present time. He (I sense him mostly as male energy) tells me that this is for about 25% or less, of the book reading population of the world. I believe if you are reading this book, you are chosen to read this at this time for a reason.

This book is about introducing a new concept in living life on earth at this present time. Yes, at this present time, where things have gone mostly out of track, and out of balance with our own personal lives, with our health, relationships, finances, careers and also our faith, belief and value systems. There is so much confusion in our everyday lives; there is much corruption in the political circles world wide - lack of strong, honest leadership and good values, natural disasters are occurring more often all over the world, crime rates have significantly increased, and all other forms of disturbances are happening around us and the world in general at this time – some would agree a period of darkness at many levels have taken over. This concept will show you how to retain your internal balance and still live a personally happy, peaceful, rewarding and meaningful life when anything and everything around you has gone out of balance.

He specifically wants me to write a very simple, and easy to understand book. From now on, I will refer to my Source as "He". I will also call him "Source" or "Creator". Although I like to address him as "God", I will consciously try not to, because I fear that people may habitually connect this to a particular religion and I want to avoid that, because it is not. The wisdom in this book belongs to Him. I am only the messenger, who is the writer here.

I absolutely love to write, I am more of a writer than a talker, but I don't consider myself as a sophisticated writer, so please don't pay attention to my writing, this is not about my writing ability. In fact, please forgive me if my writing is not perfect or up to the standards or if I have made any errors or mistakes. This book is about conveying a message to people who are ready to receive this at this time. So please pay attention to the message. I am told this is "Time Sensitive". I am told some people in the world need to see this message at this time. I wasn't told everybody in the world needs to see this. In fact, he has specifically told me not everybody will understand this concept at this time. Yes, I am very nervous about this task, so I am trying to procrastinate and find excuses, but he tells me it is time and I should not delay it any longer. In my life I have done many things for many people at different times, but this is the first time I am doing something specifically for my Creator, so I am both nervous and excited about this. But here I go – obeying the instructions of my Creator– my Source who is also my God.

As stated earlier, this book is about a particular life path – uniquely created to suite these present times. I strongly believe if you understand this concept, embrace it and decide to follow it, you can make your life more happy, peaceful, rewarding and meaningful. I believe this is a common goal we all share. I also believe this is what most of us strive to achieve in life. He put me through this path first. I actually, did not know that he was doing it, if I did I may not have agreed. I didn't have step-by-step instructions to follow like I am giving you now. It was a path I took moment to moment with lots of faith, trust and belief in him. It took me many years to get to where I am today. He certainly wanted me to experience it first, and now he is instructing me to share this with others who are open to this concept. I can confidently say, I have gone through it - or more correctly say, I have been "put-though the experiences". I now, understand this journey was for a specific purpose. It certainly was not about me, but something bigger for the benefit of others. This path certainly worked well for me, I am a very different person today in many ways, and my life has changed tremendously for the betterment and I sincerely hope this also works for you too.

I know there are hundreds of books written on numerous life paths, I have also read many over the years, however, I do believe this concept brings that piece I thought was missing in most of the books I read – I will let you experience it and decide it for yourself. Since then I have also as a Life Coach, taught this life concept as a 12 week course to some. As a pilot project, I offered these both as in-house and as an on-line program. This experience helped me to put this concept together as a step-by-step, practical, doable, achievable process.

Discover Your TRUE Self and Live Your BEST Life TODAY!

Our time on earth is really precious. There is so much to do, see and also be; and also numerous books on this topic are written by renowned writers of the world. Why would you spend your time to read this book by a no-name writer? Furthermore, why would you buy this book? What's in it for you?

I am sure you have these questions in mind; I know it because I too have such questions before purchasing something or spending my time on anything. For the majority of us, our money and time are both limited and the choices available are unlimited.

So let me ask you these questions. The answers are for yourself. It will assist you to decide for yourself if you need to purchase this book, or even read this.

- ☐ Are you mostly **satisfied** with your present life?
- ☐ Do you know the **meaning of LIFE for yourself**?
- ☐ Are you mostly **happy** with your life?
- ☐ Do you know what **"Happiness"** really means to you?
- ☐ Are you living up to your **fullest potential**?
- ☐ Are you utilizing your **Natural Gifts and Talents** to make your life better?
- ☐ Do you know **what your** Natural Gifts and Talents are?
- ☐ Are you living a **fulfilling, meaningful, rewarding** life?
- ☐ Do you know who **your Source/Creator of Life** is?
- ☐ Are you **connected** to your Source/Creator of Life?
- ☐ Do you know **your purpose** on earth?
- ☐ Do you have **peace-of-mind** about how your life is flowing?

If you answered "YES" to all questions that is fantastic. You don't really need to buy this book; it will be a total waste of your money.

If you answered "NO" to one or a few questions here, you might benefit from reading this book.

Let's be sure. Let's look at this in another angle.

- ☐ Are you feeling *restless and anxious* about your life?
- ☐ Are you feeling *overwhelmed* about your life?
- ☐ Are you feeling *lost* in your life?
- ☐ Are you feeling *empty* in your life?
- ☐ Are you feeling *confused* about your life?
- ☐ Are you feeling there should be more to life but *don't really know what that is*?
- ☐ Are you feeling like you are *missing something* in your life?

This time if you answered "NO" to all questions, you have got it great and congratulations. You have mastered it! Good Luck and Best Wishes and go do your thing and continue to shine bright. Don't buy this book. But if you still can, read it.

However, if you had at least one "YES" or a few you may want to read this book. If you do not want to buy it, borrow it from someone.

I am helping you to assess why you need to read this book. As an adult educator, I always like to set out objectives before I teach, so that the learners know why they have to invest their time or money in learning or doing something. Why are you in class and why not somewhere else? Same way I ask, why are you reading this book and why not read another book? Or do something else?

Great! So you have decided to read this book. I also think you are chosen to read this book at this time and therefore, may this book be a blessing to you and your precious life.

This is what the Source wants you to get from this book:

- Discover a path to live a better life on earth at this time – **this path is about living your BEST life NOW on earth at this present time**

- Become the **BEST YOU!**
- Discover who your Source/Creator is for you and **receive your personal blueprint** to living your best life on earth
- Discover your natural **gifts and talents** and use it to fulfill your life purpose
- Discover your **purpose on earth** and live life on purpose
- Understand you are here on earth at this time because **you are wanted and needed** and discover your **special part to play** to make this a **better world**
- Live a more **fulfilled, meaningful, rewarding everyday life**
- Live your life with **peace-of-mind, joy, simplicity, gratitude and inner happiness**
- **Consciously choose** your partnerships, relationships, projects, activities and other involvements in life – because your time here is limited and the energy you have is also limited
- Discover your path to **"Self-Actualization"** – become the person you came here to be

What is Self Actualization?

https://en.wikipedia.org/wiki/Self-actualization

The term was used by Abraham Maslow in his article, "A Theory of Human Motivation". Maslow explicitly defines **self-actualization** to be "the desire for **self-fulfillment**, namely the tendency for him [the individual] to become **actualized** in what he is potentially.

In other words, self-actualization is not about making the most money, or becoming the most famous person in the world. Instead, self-actualization is about reaching one's personal potential, whether that means becoming a singer, painter, writer, a politician, a philosopher, a teacher, or anything else. Become the person who came here to be.

As per the guidance I have received, I will try my best to make this message simple and direct. He says no "fluff" – just simple and direct. Perhaps that is why he chose me, because I only know to write simple and direct. As an English-as-a Second Language speaker and writer, I don't know enough words to create fluff even if I sometimes would like to. I hope my lack becomes a blessing.

How to use this book:

I invite you to read this book with an open mind. I know the readers of this book are not born yesterday; this means you already come with many concepts, beliefs, views, opinions, etc. And I am not pouring water to an empty bucket, and likely the bucket is filled with a lot of accumulations from past. Therefore, you would benefit if you read this book with an open mind. This book is about **YOU and YOUR life**. From time to time, when appropriate I will share my experiences but the **focus is on YOU**. So get some highlighters and markers if you need. Underline or highlight if you wish. Write on the pages or margins if you like. Be fully engaged. Read to understand, and not just to gather more and more information. Take time to reflect upon what you read. Ask yourself, would this concept help me to make my present life better?

Lets get started shall we?

Many of us today are living hopelessly and aimlessly. Many of us are not connected with our inner selves anymore and therefore do not know who we really are. Our identity is based on what others say or think about us. So we are operating out of a false or distorted identity. We pursue life aimlessly, often following other people's agendas, chasing success and happiness purely based on what is defined by others. Pursuing things, people and projects that does not give us any satisfaction or fulfilment. We want to be happy but do not know what happiness really mean to us. Same way, we want to be successful, but do not know what success really means to us personally. We claim we are "super busy" in life: our agendas are full. But we are very tired living everyday life – going home only to "drop dead on our couches", dreaming of the arrival of Friday – then not knowing what happened to the weekend, hating Mondays; there is no sense of peace, joy or tranquility but constantly wondering why we are feeling this way. Most of us are running, but where are we running to? What are we chasing? Nobody seems to know, but we continue to run. From the time we wake up until we fall asleep, we are running, exhausted and depleted. And, many of us do this again and again and again.

Even with numerous degrees and diplomas in our hands we are empty; I see no lack of education, the colleges and universities are full with learners - many of us have become experts of this or that, we pride ourselves on our knowledge of the outside world, we are masters of so many things, we explore the world we live endlessly, and now we have also started to explore other worlds, but we still don't know what touches our own hearts and souls. How well do you know yourself? Who are you really? What is the purpose of life? We go to school to learn line dancing or to decorate cupcakes or to learn computers, but when do we go to school to learn about us? Aren't you the most important person in your life? Do you know enough about you? Who are YOU? Who are you really?

Relationships no longer have any meaning, and is not rewarding, with so many equipment and apps to stay connected we are still feeling lonely and isolated; smart phone, iPad, Facebook, messenger, twitter, snapchat, texting, e-mailing, - all these are supposed to connect us to people, we claim we have hundreds and sometimes thousands of friends in our Facebook accounts but yet we don't feel connected to anyone. More and more of us are crossing the roads, eating dinner at restaurants and riding buses, trains and air planes and even driving while trying to connect to people all over the world. We panic if we could not check our e-mails or voice mails for ten minutes. But with all these connections at the end of the day so many of us still feel isolated, lost and abandoned. Depression, anxiety, stress and suicide rates are rising all over the world. Who are we really trying to connect with?

Furthermore, we are completely disconnected from our SOURCE - Source? Who is that? Or what is that? Who gives us real Love? Power? Wisdom? Guidance? Protection? Security? Who or what gives us energy to live? Who or what gives us purpose? Why are we here on earth? What are we suppose to achieve or accomplish on our short journey between birth and death?

Discover your TRUE self and live your BEST life Today (DYTS and LYBLT) is designed to connect you and align yourself with your inner self – your TRUE self, your SOURCE and your LIFE PURPOSE. When you are aligned with these three you are able to perform at your highest potential. He reminds me you were created to perform at this level - This is about living your BEST life NOW at this present time; this is not about trying to create a successful afterlife; this is about living your very best life now on earth at this time with purpose and meaning and becoming a contributor to make this earth a better place for you and others.

So in this book we will focus on three essential phases:

Phase 1:   Taking you on an **Inward** Journey to connect you with your inner self

Phase 2:   Taking you on an **Upward** Journey to connect you with your Source/Creator

Phase 3:   Taking you on an **Outward** Journey to connect you with the outside world

Phase 1:   Taking you on an Inward Journey to connect you with your inner self

The primary focus of this phase is to provide opportunities for SELF DISCOVERY to find your TRUE SELF. Do you know yourself enough? Do you know what you stand for in life? Do you know what your Values and Beliefs are? Are your values and beliefs aligned with the life you want to live? Are they helping you or hindering you? You may lead a busy and hectic life but are you really following your own agenda or are you chasing after someone else's? Are you on the right path? Or are you on someone else's path? Are you going where you want to go or are you been dragged to go somewhere else?

What does happiness really mean to you? What does success really mean to you? What does love mean to you? What do you really want to do with your life? What are your dreams and goals? What is stopping you from growing? Where are you stuck? What are your limitations and barriers? Are you living the life that you are meant to be living? Are you fulfilling your goals and dreams? Learn to understand, appreciate and accept your own unique self. Live your life up to your fullest potential. Learn about yourself, the most important person in your life. Understand yourself clearly, know what you want, know what you have and go for your goals.

I would say, this is the heaviest phase out of the three. This is also where I spent most of my time - learning and discovering about my own self. This is also the heaviest phase, when teaching this course. Most of the sessions were spent here. A lot of digging and probing was needed. Some areas were not easy or fun, but most of the growth happened here. The self-awareness I received through this phase helped me to let go many unhealthy accumulations I was carrying. It de-cluttered my life. It helped me become lighter. It is essential you complete this phase before you move to the next.

Phase 2: Taking you on an Upward Journey to connect you with your Source/Creator

Who is your Source/Creator? Who gives you life? Who gives you purpose? This is not a religious question but you could have a religious answer and it is perfectly okay. I am not here to teach you any religion because I don't know enough about any religion. Some readers may know the answer to this question instantly. And some may not. Some may have to think. And some may change their original answers after they read this book. None of you are wrong. Where ever you are, just accept yourself because this is where you need to be. This is not about proving anything to anyone. This is about discovering your own unique path to meeting your Source.

Ever wonder why you are here on earth? What are you really suppose to do with your life? We come to earth and also leave earth with no material possessions. And we are all here for a short period of time. Our existence on earth, is it just about us or are we part of a bigger plan? Make a connection with your Source/Creator and find out why you are here. Identify your Creator given Gifts and Talents to live your best life. Honour your life purpose and start to live a more meaningful, rewarding and productive everyday life. When you are connected with your Source, you will receive your own unique blueprint to life. Who you are and why you are here will make sense. You will understand why you are the way you are and will start to accept who you are just the way you are. This is the phase you find your perfect alignment. This is where you will find the entry way to your unique path to life. This is the missing piece I was always looking for in my search for the real purpose of life. Many books and courses I took in the past helped me to understand who I am but I didn't know why I am here and what I am suppose to do with who I am. This is where I felt like I found the perfect glove that fitted me. I found this phase truly liberating. This gave me a clear picture of my unique path to life.

Phase 3: Taking you on an Outward Journey to connect you with the outside world

Here, you take the time to understand the different roles you play and its importance and meaning to your present life. Here, I learnt to evaluate my relationships and partnerships in life, and consciously chose to hold on to partnerships that contributed to the betterment of my life. I learnt to let go relationships, projects and activities that no longer served me.

This is where I realized that I have been walking on the wrong path with wrong people for many years. Prior to learning about this phase, my life was primarily focused on my relationships and partnerships with the external world. I was bound to them by tradition, custom or culture. It didn't take me anywhere fruitful or rewarding; it didn't give me fulfilment or meaning in life. I also did not have a relationship with myself or my Creator. I didn't know who I was and what was important to me, I relied a lot on external sources to tell me who I am or what is important for me. I relied on the external relationships to give me meaning and purpose, I depended a lot on others to fill me with love, peace, happiness, joy, self worth, etc. I was constantly looking for someone to complete me and validate me. My self-worth was purely based on what others thought of me, or spoke of me. I had a huge inner void and constantly looked for external sources to fill it. I realized I gave simply to receive. Sometimes I gave and gave until I had absolutely nothing to give. Most times I ran empty. I spend most of my energy, time and resources on nurturing others so that they could nurture me.

In the following chapters we will go deeper into these phases.

Please be patient with yourself. Please do not expect instant success and dramatic results right away. You can expect subtle, gradual changes in your outlook on life over a period of weeks or even months. With regular reflection and practice, things will start to happen. This is a learning curve you need to master in your own time and not a competition.

May I please remind you to approach this with an open mind? Take time to reflect, think and question your learning.

Are you ready?

Phase One

Taking you on an Inward Journey to connect you with your Inner Self

We will now journey inwards to meet your Truest Self – your Inner Self. He tells me we are all created and delivered into this world as true, unique individuals and we are never to be compared with another. We are crafted uniquely and made specifically on purpose for a very special reason.

Please know, you are exactly where you need to be at this very moment. Depending on where you are, it may be hard for you to believe but I am asked to tell you this. This is where you start your journey, but not necessarily where you will end. You could be in a rough or dark spot right now, but you can still start this inward journey today. You do not have to wait for a sunny day. Your past is not a barrier for you to take this journey inwards.

What is needed is your permission and willingness to take this journey. And remember; only you can do this for yourself and no one else can.

So are you ready? Come, walk with me, I will show you the way – **the way he has shown me.**

You carry a Diamond

I am told, when we arrive on earth we each come with a "Diamond" that is raw and unpolished. This diamond is the core of ourselves, our purest selves; this is where our true worth resides. You may imagine this as a microchip in a computer. This is where everything you need to live your BEST life is stored. Yes, everything you need to live your life on purpose is already provided for you - your unique purpose in life is embedded in this diamond along with the wisdom, knowledge and tools you need to fulfill this purpose. Where ever you are in life, regardless how old you are or what sort of life circumstances you are facing at this present moment, you are a unique human being with a unique life purpose and your purpose in life is in this diamond. It is in you and inside of you. You will forever hold this diamond with you and no one can take it away from you. Other people's influence can hide its true light but no one can really take it away from you. It is yours and yours only.

You are a Coffee Cup!

Now, imagine yourself as a cup. Yes a disposable coffee cup. Visualize all of us as coffee cups, you, me and everybody else, in your family and your life circle, where ever you are in this world, which ever country you live in, man or woman or any other way you identify - white, black, brown, yellow – in the eyes of the Creator, you are nothing but a coffee cup! Yes, Oprah Winfrey, Barack Obama, Mahatma Gandhi, Mohammad Ali, Tom Cruise, Princess Diana – then you and me, we are all coffee cups. As mentioned our cup comes with a "Diamond" and our purpose in life is to polish this diamond and make it shine as best as possible. Each person is created for a unique purpose and has a unique path to walk on, no two individuals are created the same and we each have our own path to walk on and our special purpose to achieve.

Got it? This is how we came to this world.

By the way, he reminds me that we only have ONE cup, no one gets two, everyone gets only one cup. You can be rich, famous, powerful, highly influential, have royal blood, or a celebrity of the world - but you still have only one cup. You cannot exchange your cup with another, nor can you buy a new one if it becomes damaged. We have to accept the cup we receive. The state of this cup sometimes may not always be perfect; sometimes it can be dented, or broken on delivery or even after. Some may have a larger cup and some small, but bottom line is we only get one. I hope you get the idea. Precious isn't it?

Your Internal Operating System - IOS

From the minute we arrive on planet earth, others around us start to throw labels at our cup – it usually starts with the gender – is it a boy or girl? Then it moves to the birth order - eldest, middle, youngest, then it moves to skin colours – light, dark, etc., each living moment, these labels keep growing just like bacteria. Who is throwing these labels at us? Others! Who are these others? It can be our parents, grand parents, relatives, teachers, religious leaders, neighbours, friends, and media and collectively we can call them "Society". Who is society – everybody else other than yourself! Day after day, year after year, our cup gets filled with more and more labels. As soon as we become toddlers, or even before - these labels will start to dictate our lives: we are told how to be, how to think, how to do, what to do, where to go, etc. Our cups get filled with labels that we have to live up to, but didn't really choose. By the time we become ten, our Internal Operating System (IOS) is developed, yes! Just like a computer, we too have an internal operating system. This system dictates us and controls us. This is a system fed by others – the society, but it will start to control us and define who we are. We will live our lives with the commands made by this operating system. But, yet our true identity and life purpose is in the diamond. We never get a chance to explore it. By the time, we graduate from high school, that original diamond we came with is nowhere to be seen. In addition, it is possible we do not even know that we have a diamond inside of us. How can we know? Our school system does not talk about this. Likely majority don't even know this. Society also does not educate us on this. Therefore, it is neglected and it gets buried deeper and deeper by the day. By the time we are twenty-five, we are now cups full of "crap" and we do not even know it. Isn't it really sad?

As you can see, our thinking, actions and behaviour becomes commands of this operating system built by others. Based on these commands, we make decisions;

some very important life decisions – such as our professions, if or not we should get married, if or not we should have children, where we should live, what we should become, etc. An operating system that is truly not ours dictates us. Yes, an operating system that is not ours becomes our default operating system and controls our life. Scary isn't it? Does this make sense to you? **Who we are and how we become who we are in life?**

Our personal identity is built based on this operating system which consists of many labels; labels that we really didn't choose. We often take pride in introducing ourselves to others based on this false identity – we hold on to these labels that we didn't really create. Sometimes we literally kill ourselves to hold on to these labels – don't we? Many of us spend the rest of our lives proving to the world we are these labels even though we may know we are not. But is this your TRUEST self? Who are you really when these labels are taken away from you?

Journey Inwards

Now this is where our task begins, we journey inwards into our coffee cups, searching for that diamond; it is in the very bottom because that is where it was placed at the time of our birth. Remember, the cup was empty when we came here. So now we have to dive to the bottom of it to find the diamond and this means to go through all the labels that it is covered with. May I remind you, this may not be easy? It is normal to want to skip this part but, please do not skip here. Be courageous and take this journey further inwards because it is for your own betterment. Once you complete this journey, you will agree that this is the best gift you can give for yourself. Having completed this, I can say it is truly worth it. It purifies you and simplifies your life completely. Yes, it is like taking a strong detox – and it may not be a pleasant experience but we have to remember that it is good for us. After this process, my life changed so much and the change was like night and day. And it was certainly a "positive" change. For me, this is the best thing I ever did for myself. I sincerely hope you will agree with me in time.

Hunt for the Diamond begins

While we start on the hunt to search for the diamond, let us consciously be kind to ourselves. This is not a time to point fingers at others or yourself. We need to approach this with much love, kindness and patience.

Depending on where you are in life, for some this "cleaning-up process" will be easy, but for some others may not be. This book is written to a "self-help" audience but if this becomes too daunting for you, please get the appropriate support you need. You may consider seeking the support of a good Life Coach, Family Counsellor or a Therapist.

4 Corner-Pillars and Life Stage

As you dive inwards to examine the labels – you will see all the "invisible stuff" you have accumulated over the years. These accumulated "invisible stuff" can be categorized mainly as the 4 Corner-Pillars of your Life Stage. Our life stage is supported by the following 4 Corner-Pillars:

- Values and Beliefs
- Life Principles/Rules/Regulations
- Culture/Traditions/Habits/Customs
- Social Expectations/Obligations

It is on this "Life Stage" we perform our daily life that consists of different roles. We become who we are based on the influences of what is stored in these

4 corner-pillars. We all come to this world as human babies – nothing but humans, but because of the heavy influence of these external labels we are seen as different to each. It is because of these labels we start to look at people differently and treat them differently. This is where the separation is created. Isn't this phenomenal? Take time to reflect. What if these labels never existed? How different our world would be? Look at the world of flora and fauna? Does a Sunflower know that it is called a Sunflower? Does a Rose know that it is called a Rose? Yet they blossom so beautifully and happily next to each other!

Let us take the value of gender; we say to a little boy of five years old "boys are smarter than girls". This little boy will take this value in without thinking because he does not have reasoning ability at this age. He has no filters; no boundaries. If we say this enough times, he starts to believe this and it gets planted in his default system. As a teenager, now this is firmly planted in his system, he will not question it unless he is given an opportunity. For many of us, this means never! He turns to an adult and makes important decisions based on this value. He will see women as weak or not as strong as men, because it is in his default thinking. He will continue to act based on this initial value that is planted in his system.

This is the same with every other value or belief we hold in our system. It is also the same with the rest of the three corner-pillars of our life stage - Does this make sense? Profound isn't it? Based on these labels we actually become who we are. If we don't consciously come out of this, we will spend our entire lives trying to fit in with these labels somebody else stuck on us. Many of us for generations have already done this. Should we continue to live our lives this way? Or should we do something about it? It is your decision. He tells me this.

Most of us are used to an education system that is "fed" into us, very few of us were taught or even given the opportunity to question or think. Things are generally stuffed into our systems saying it is needed to live a successful life. But there is a lot of stuff we really don't want or need at this present time. This stuff weighs us down, creates separation and animosity within us. Not only do we not need or want them, they are hindering our progress in life. We continue to accumulate all kinds of "stuff"- stuff that we expect to give us joy or peace; we spend our entire lives to chase after these things that we think we cant live without, then finally when the "curtain call" comes and when we are forced to hop into our death beds we wish we lived differently. We wish we pursued what we really loved and lived more simply and joyfully. This has been our pattern now for a long time – perhaps centuries. Why are we doing this again and again? Should you end this now when you can? Is this the time to change? I will let you answer this question for yourself, because this is about **YOUR life**. Take your time to reflect on this. This is big. It's a decision you have to make.

I hope you decide to consider change – not for anyone but for yourself!

As you can see, our systems are stuffed with so much trash. Things that others at one time thought were important and valuable for them. Perhaps they were, at that time but is it for you now? Much space is taken for unwanted stuff that clutters our minds and thinking. We need to get rid of what is not needed anymore. Therefore, we need to clean-up our systems just like a computer loaded with unwanted apps and programs. This is what this concept is introducing, an opportunity to clean-up our systems. Yes, Discover Your True Self and Live your Best Life Today (DYTS & LYBLT) is here to clean-up your system – will help you to look at your cup, get rid of what you no longer need and make your cup cleansed, simplified and clutter free. It will also help you free up space to install any new things you want to include in your present life – yes just like a computer!

At this stage what the Source is requesting you to do here is to look at these "labels" or "stuff" and ask yourself if this is something you need to continue to hold on to. If you think, you should then keep it. But this time, you are doing this with responsibility and ownership. Keep things you still need and value, and let everything else go.

How do you decide if something is valuable to you or not?

A question to ask yourself:

- *By holding this (value, belief, life principle, rule, regulation, culture, habit, custom, tradition, social expectation, obligation) has it helped me to become a better person? Or is it hindering my progress of becoming the person I want to be?*

If it is helping you, keep it. If not, let it go.

Here are some other ways to ask this question;

- *Is it giving me positive energy or is it draining me?*
- *Is this a contributor or a contaminator to my present life?*

You can follow this same process in all areas - Values and Beliefs, Life Principles, Culture/Traditions/Habits/Customs and Social Expectations and Obligations. May I remind you to continue to remain with kindness and compassion to yourself during this process as it will require some time. Please do not expect overnight results. Give yourself the time you need. Don't rush but also please don't skip.

What are you stuffed with?

Now I am going to ask you to pay attention to some common terms, and please take your time reflecting them for yourself. This activity is to cleanse your coffee cup further. After cleansing you will feel much relief but while you are cleansing it, may not be the same. Because you have to deal with the dirt, the grease and the grime – so be patient with the process. Imagine yourself cleaning a precious appliance that is full of dirt. You want to clean the appliance because it is precious and has value to you, and you cannot afford to throw it away, because it is one of a kind and it is all you have. But you now have to clean the dirt. The process is not fun but it is essential. However, once you clean it up you will feel happy and accomplished because you have high value for it.

Here, we will look at some popular terms – common social terms to most - could be discovered within the 4 corner-pillars of your life stage, which you learnt as a child that helped you shape who you are today. And now, we look at its true significance for you today. It is about how you perceive these terms today in your life. In my in-house or on-line program, I allow 6 weeks to work on these. So take your time. Don't rush. Here is the list; we will reflect on terms such as:

Success	Lust	Partnership	Support
Happiness	Abuse	Responsibility	Citizenship
Failure	Marriage	Boundaries	Voting
Life	Divorce	Friendship	Right
Death	Mother	Home	Wrong
Human	Father	Religion	Good
Gender	Husband	God	Bad
Freedom	Wife	Spirituality	Words
Power	Children	Soul	Thoughts

Wealth	Family	Faith	Action
Money	Parent	Fun	Leadership
Achievement	Romance	Security	Politics
Education	Sex	Protection	Business
Respect	Sexuality	Guidance	Man
Love	Intimacy	Fear	Woman

Can you think any more? The list can go on. Reflect on the meaning, value and importance of these terms in your life. If it helps, think of the images that come to your mind, or the symbols or the signs or even the colours that associates the above. Feel free to add to your list, depending your need. It is likely you may have first heard many of these terms/words when you were under ten. For most of us, formal definitions/perceptions may have formed later in life with actual life experiences.

Yes, I admit, this is an exhausting process, especially the more older we are the more harder, because the value and meaning for above is heavily influenced with our – culture, traditions, customs, views, opinions, habits, etc. But it is very important to go through this process. Please trust me on this and continue to walk with me. Here, you are examining the meanings and value of these for yourself, **not for anyone but for yourself**, you decide what it means to you today and its value in your life, in this present time. Perhaps this is the very first time in your life you are doing this, and yes it can be hard and may even feel strange.

When I was doing this for the first time, it was daunting. My perception of Success, Happiness, Life, Marriage, Divorce, Sex, God, Spirituality, Religion and more – all these have a very different significance to me today at this present time. I no longer hold on to the traditional perception I was fed-into as a child. Many of the terms mean very different to me today at where I stand, and this realization has completely changed me and how I view my present life. For an example my initial meaning of marriage meant the partnership was forever. But over the years, through my own life experiences I realized that marriage is not forever and if the partnership is not working, one must allow it to end. I also see ending of a marriage as not the end of life. I was stuck in an unfruitful, unpleasant marriage for 25 years. This initial meaning/ understanding of marriage, which was implanted in me as a child was in my default operating system and was dictating me. This combination of value, belief and traditional meaning did not allow me to end a marriage that no longer served me in my best interests. In reality it made my life miserable. It made me sick physically, emotionally and spiritually. It was hindering me and drained me and did not allow me to grow as a person; it stopped me from achieving my fullest potential. But through this process I realized I no longer hold on to that thought, value or belief. The traditional meaning of marriage that was implanted in my default system no longer serves my best interests. If I did not engage in this process I would have not realized this for myself. This realization was a true eye-opener. A huge liberator and a total cleanser. So please don't be afraid to assess your situation. Give new meaning to things that you need. May I remind you this is your life and you owe this to yourself? I was trapped in something painful and unproductive for long period of time. I knew it didn't serve me well but I could not let go because of some values that was implanted in my default system. Once I examined it I realized that the values I was holding on to were outdated and it no longer had any significance to my present life. Hope this makes sense to you.

Another example is Success – success to me as a child was living a certain life –having a certain type of body image, being a certain person affiliated with a professional title, holding a high ranking position in a corner office with a view, married to a certain type of a person, raising children, driving a certain type of car, associating certain type of people, living in a certain type of home in a certain type of neighbourhood; this is the picture of success that was painted on me by society. For more than seventy five percent of my life, I strived to achieve this and I am not ashamed to admit, I killed myself to achieve and maintain this – but I could not, I did not even come closer to this. I tried but it didn't work for me. I failed terribly. I now realize I was chasing someone else's definition of success. It was not mine. I did not feel passionate about what I was chasing. I realized success meant very different things to me. Today success means living life on purpose, doing what I love to do - utilizing my Creator given gifts and talents, forming meaningful relationships, contributing to the society in a positive way, engaging in activities and projects that touches my heart, being able to stand on my two feet, living my life with passion, joy, peace-of-mind, simplicity and gratitude – this is what Success means to me and today I sure feel I am successful. I hope you get the picture. **This is about YOU; not anyone else.**

Please don't hold on to the original value if it does not serve you in your best interest any more. As you look at all these, you keep what still matters to you and discard what no longer serves you. Understand whatever you decide to keep - you do with responsibility and your own choice. I discovered a lot I was holding on to have no value for me in my present life. Yes, at the beginning I felt guilty to throw away these because it was something my parents or culture had taught me or said it is important. However, when I examined it in todays light, it wasn't important for me anymore. It did not make any sense for me to hold on to it anymore. It did not serve me well at this point of time in life. And most importantly it stopped me from growing and reaching my highest potential. In fact, some of them were thwarting my progress in life. I was born in a country where caste, class, religion, culture and traditions were of highest value. People kill others to protect these labels. Today, these things don't compliment the life I am living, and in fact it is thwarting me, through realization and developing awareness, I was able to completely let go of these labels. Today I only see myself as a human. And this is extremely freeing. And this realization has made my life really simple. It has broaden my view of the world.

I look at all people as humans. I am not able to change the minds of all others in the world, but I can change how I view the world for myself by changing MY mind. It feels extremely liberating to live this way. My cup is getting lighter and simpler.

After you clean up all this, down in the bottom of your cup you will find your diamond. It may not look like a diamond as it is covered with all the dirt and grime. Actually, isn't this how you find diamonds in the real world too? - buried deep in dirt? This diamond is your truest self. In it, you will also find your gifts and talents. Each cup holder comes with their unique gifts and talents for a specific reason. Not everybody has the same gifts and talents. So do not look in to other peoples' cups, only look at your own. Do not compare, we are not the same, we are unique. As humans, we are valued same but we all carry different gifts and talents for a purpose. The world is created this way for a good reason. In order for the world to operate in a balanced way, we need unique people in unique roles. Doctors are needed, but so as patients. Leaders are needed, so as followers. Artists are needed, so as street sweepers and therefore, we need to hold on to those unique gifts and talents and utilize them accordingly.

Your Natural Gifts and Talents

Please know, we each have gifts – and Yes! They are simply gifts – they are given to you by your Creator, simply placed in you –not because you are better than someone else. But because it is part of his Master Plan to keep this world in balance. These gifts come easily to you, with no struggle, they can be things like the ability to sing, to write, to play an instrument, to draw, to paint, to solve problems, to bake, to analyze, to organize, to sell, to build, to dance, to create, to teach, to talk, to listen, to lead, to perform, to direct, to cook - there are zillion different talents and combinations; sure they can be learnt, but there are people who are simply gifted. For people who are gifted it comes naturally without much effort and it always comes with a natural interest and passion. When you are gifted you are also passionate about it. The best way to notice this is by observing a toddler, there are certain talents they pickup on their own, they come to earth knowing these – they are not taught. As early as 3 or 4, I could draw and all I ever wanted was to draw – no one directed me to drawing, I picked it up on my own, and also I had incredible ability to mix colours naturally, I just knew which colours go together, again no one taught me or showed me how. Every single cup owner comes with these gifts and talents. Pay attention - you have them too. What are your natural gifts and talents? Do you know? Take some time to reflect and asses your gifts and talents. What did you do best when you were under 10 years old? If you are a parent please pay attention to your children. What do they do well naturally? Remember, these may not rank top in the commercial world or the labour market, but its valuable and we carry it because of a bigger reason.

Because of the labels we are usually stuffed with, and the pressure to live up to these labels, majority of us may not get an opportunity to discover our true gifts and talents unless we consciously stop to do so. Even when some may know about their gifts, society sometimes steer them away from these because as per society standards they may not be the right skills to have. They may be labeled as not marketable or not prestigious enough or not profitable. Growing up as a child, my father steered me away from sketching, art, music and writing, and this - I now realize because of his own fears and insecurities. Those days Artists or Musicians did not do well in life and he probably thought I would pursue art or music as a career. I don't think

I wanted to be a professional artist or a musician but I just wanted to hold on to those gifts because it gave me joy. I loved to write because it is through writing I express myself, I am not a big talker. I write more than I talk. I loved music because listening to certain types of music inspired me to reach higher aspirations for myself. Music is always the biggest inspiration for all the work I do. I now understand my father did this with the right intentions but with his limited human knowledge. But what he did not know is, it is through art, colours, music and writing, I communicate with my Source. I use sketching and colours to download information from my Source. It is my method of communication with my Source. I connect to my Source through music and also transfer his wisdom through writing. Looking back, my Creator gave me the exact talents and gifts I needed to have to live my purpose. But unfortunately, the people around me did not understand this. The very same things I needed to polish through my journey to fulfill my true purpose in life, I was steered away from. It was a struggle to retain these gifts and talents as a young child. I was not strong enough as a child to fight for these, and I gave up and lost the battle. Although the society told me I did not need these, I knew deep in my heart I really needed these. But I didn't have a voice as a child and the reasoning ability to explain it to the adults around me. I had very different gifts and talents from my siblings. Theirs was in competitive sports. I certainly was not good in sports and I had no interest or passion for it. I always disliked competition. I remember my father was worried and upset as I did not share the same talents and gifts. Unfortunately my gifts and talents went unrecognized simply because they were different from others. Sadly it became my loss. So if you are a parent please be mindful of this. Even though unintentional, you might destroy something very valuable.

For some, it's possible they never knew they had these gifts. But he tells me, everybody has gifts and talents. So allow yourself to discover these gifts and talents – to notice, to identify, to accept and to embrace these gifts and talents as Creator given. This is an important part of your true identity. Part of your true identity lies in these gifts and talents. These are your true assets; they will always remain with you. No one can take it away from you. They are not subjected to any outside influences – the economy, labour market fluctuations, inflation, job loss, relationship breakdowns, weather, political influences – these will always remain with you. You may have not yet discovered them but they are there – inside of you.

Weaknesses, Barriers and Limitations

Same way, we also come with barriers and limitations – no single person is free of this. This is where we get to grow and learn. Your weakness allows another to serve and shine. Imagine you as the student, you are going to school to work on your weaknesses, and the teacher is there with her strengths to serve you. This partnership is already created. Isn't it amazing? Take a moment to realize this pattern for yourself. The doctor and the patient, the leader and the follower - there is a reason for everything. There is a rhythm and pattern in us and around us, in the entire universe – this extends to all and everything – to us humans, the animals, the trees, the mountains, sky, the rivers and the oceans and even the tiniest little insects. We are all here because we are all needed for this "Show" on earth called "Life". We all have a part to play. The "Curtain Call" can come anytime, but until then we perform. Profound isn't it? This wisdom was just downloaded to me as I write, I feel awed by this. I will take a moment to thank him for this wisdom. Take some time to reflect. Because it is huge. Understanding this will truly liberate you. It will free you from the constant battle to strive to survive. We no longer need to strive just to survive, but we need to strive to live our lives fully and completely; with true joy and authenticity. He tells me we are here to enjoy life here on earth. And we are encouraged to utilize our gifts to make this earth beautiful and better for self and others.

Do you realize that we are created this way for a reason, and our barriers and limitations are also for a reason? And that we are all perfectly and thoughtfully created this way? And we have absolutely no need to compare ourselves with another or feel inferior? We also don't need to strive to survive anymore, because we all come with a departure date, that is unavoidable, and none of us are getting out of this show alive. Sooner or later, the curtain call is going to come, and no one is spared from this. Absolutely no one. So why kill ourselves to survive, what we need to do is to live as best as we could with what we have in this moment. This realization makes my heart full of glee. How liberating is this?

Somethings you can't have?

He tells me that you will also have at least one thing you really want but can't have. Look around, everybody does. This is to show you that nothing or no one is 100% perfect. Something I always wanted in my life was a happily married life. I always wanted this ever since I was sixteen. Likely because of the all the "Harlequin" and "Mills and Boons" romances I read, I wanted a Prince Charming to come save me. I dreamt of a certain happily married life just like in those movies. But deep down in my core I always knew that I was not supposed to get married. I had this very clear, flash when I was nineteen. But I did not know how to interpret that signal. I got married when I was 25 and really tried to make it work for 25 more years. I carried a marriage that was meant for two, just by myself because it was my dream. I was in love with love. I don't think it was the other person's dream. Now I understand when we say it needs two people to tango. When I look back, and where I am now – I understand why marriage was not for me. My Source had a different plan for me. So look in your life, you may also have something that you really want but can't achieve. We live in a world where we are constantly told we can have everything we want. So it's very tempting to want to achieve everything we want. But, can we? There is no harm in trying but if you are repeatedly failing even with your hard work and good intentions – take a step back and review and reflect. Perhaps it is not in your plan. Listen to life messages and signs you are receiving. If you look, you will see. If you listen, you will hear. When I look back, the signs were there very clearly. But I did not pay attention.

Your Role Models

Who are your Role Models? They play a very important part in our lives. Our role models shape our lives in a big way; sometimes positively and sometimes negatively too. Now that you know better do you want to hold on to any who influence you in a negative way? Who were your role models in the past and who are they now? Have they changed over the years? Keep the ones you still treasure and let others go. I noticed, certain people I considered as Role Models years ago are still important to me today. I still value them and admire them. So I will keep them. But I also have new role models that I value and appreciate. My present top Role Models are Oprah Winfrey, Michelle Obama and Joyce Meyer. I have never met these people in person but I am drawn to them like a magnet, their work truly inspires me and motivates me. I share some of their interests, passions, values and beliefs in life. These three women also share their personal challenges openly in the world. Through their powerful and incredible stories I have learnt a lot. Although I have never met these women I feel I have a close connection to these women way more than I have with my own family. Sure, I don't meet them at family gatherings or afternoon tea, but through social media and television I get to learn about their work on a regular basis. These women have contributed immensely to shape my present life. Their presence in this world and the work they do are valuable to me, and I treasure them very much. We may never meet in real life, but they have made a huge positive impact in my life. So keep the ones you still love, value and need in your present life. Remember, we don't need to fill our cups with unwanted stuff anymore. Our goal is to keep it simple, clean and clutter free.

Your Ideal or Dream Life

Here we will pause to look at your ideal or Dream life. What is your ideal life? Is it different from your present life? Is there a huge gap between your ideal life and your present life? Can you make your ideal life your real life? What are the important segments of your ideal life? – this could be areas such as career, family, relationships, significant other, health, finances, recreation, hobbies and interests, home, physical space, community or volunteer work, personal and spiritual development, etc. Take a realistic inventory of what is really working well in each area of your present life. Keep the areas you still want and value in your present life, also assess to see if things are working as per your liking. What can you do to make things better? Let go those aspects of life you no longer want or need with love and respect. When we let go of the unwanted then we create new space for the things we love and want to embrace. What do you need to make your life closer to your ideal life? Also ask yourself, the life that you want to live, is it your dream or does it belong to someone else? Do you still want to hold on to a dream that belongs to someone else? Or do you want to create something for yourself? Assess and reflect: What is rewarding and meaningful to you? Include more of those. What is draining and exhausting? Can you get rid of these things? I have started to live more and more closer to living my dream life. It is no longer a dream; it is becoming my real life. The hope and possibility of achieving things are becoming lot more real than before. But before I got to this stage I had to let go of all the unwanted clutter. Sure! It was a lot of work, but it was worth it.

Creating space for NEW things you want and like

All these assignments are created so your internal operating system is properly cleaned-up and all viruses or as many as you could is removed, so that you have the most up-to- date operating system. Just like with a computer, this process will also free up space to install new apps and programs - such as new values or beliefs. "My Self" is a new aspect I included in my life. I realise I grew up without having a sense of self. My life did not have space for self. I was everything to others but was nothing to myself. Self-Love, Self-Care, Self-Confidence, Self-Protection, Self-Respect, Self-Worth, Self-Awareness, Self-Knowledge, Self-Satisfaction, Self Honesty - these are new terms I added to my new vocabulary. With my old operating system, the programming was done by the society. However, it became my default operating system controlling my life all this time. And now I got a chance to create my own operating system. Yes, it's a lot of work but it is worth it. I consider it a huge achievement. It is the best thing that happened to me.

As mentioned earlier, the main focus of this concept is to give you a chance to look within. This concept gives you another chance at life. This gives you an opportunity for you to connect with your True Self - The True Self your Creator created with a unique purpose in mind.

Creating Personal Boundaries

I hope your cup is now cleansed and you were able to get rid of all the unnecessary accumulations. I hope you are feeling good about what is in your cup and you are holding on to things because you simply want to and you value them. Once you do this then you need to put a lid on your cup. Yes, visualize a disposable coffee cup with a lid. This is where you install your own security system, with personal boundaries. Imagine all the safety and security systems we utilize to protect our homes, cars, computers and even our phones. We do numerous things to protect our physical body – wearing a safety jacket, gloves, helmet, goggles, kneepads, etc. Now how can we protect our precious Inner Self? What do we do to protect our one and only cup? From now on, you will take the responsibility to protect your cup and ensure you keep it free from viruses, hackers and invaders. Remember, it is your only cup. Once you install the lid, you will decide when you are going to open the lid and for whom. There maybe times in life that you may want to open the lid just a little, just for that single sip.

There are times you may want to open the whole lid of your cup – to welcome things and people. You can also imagine this as the front door to your home. Just like a peep-hole on your front door – sometimes, before you open you want to check who is out there – you don't always want to fully open your inner door to anyone and everyone. You want to be mindful as to whom you allow in your Inner World. So you can decide when you want to open yourself fully – you would do this with your inner circle – things or people that bring you positive, vibrant energy. And then there may be times when you want to keep it completely closed such as with things or people that bring in negative or toxic energy. This is about choosing to live life with mindfulness. You become conscious of your life, being present in the moment. Just like a computer, from now on - you will no longer say "yes" to auto updates to your life, you will manually agree to install the updates only if it serves you well. Why clutter your life with unnecessary things? Just like a computer why install apps and programs you really don't need or have any use? When a computer is overloaded with programs the run time becomes very slow. Same way, when we overload our life with unnecessary things, people, projects and activities it slows us down, we are constantly busy, running around, tired, exhausted and depleted – it takes away our precious and limited energy from living authentically. And may I remind you? We are here on earth for a very short time. Take time to reflect.

YOU as a member of a Human

My Source also wants you to have a clearer understanding of yourself as a human. You are a human. As a human, we can control certain things but not everything. If we go back on what we learnt, everything in your 4 corner-pillars you can control and change – because these are installed by other humans around you. So your values, beliefs, life principles, rules, regulations, traditions, customs, habits, social expectations, and obligations can be changed. If you wish, with your willingness you can change the entire life stage you perform on. You can build a new life stage if you want. You are in control of these changes, you may have not realized this before but you have control here. If you are willing you can change. Nothing is carved in stone and all of these things are, just labels created by society. **By shifting your mind, you can shift everything! This is a power and ability you have as a human.**

Human Limitations

There are certain things in life we cannot change or control. It is important we understand this very clearly. For example, we can organize an outdoor event several months in advance and on the day of the event we could experience severe weather. We cannot control nature - We cannot really control the sunset or the sunrise - pause here to reflect on things you cannot control as a human. If needed make a list. Can we eliminate Death? Aging? Sickness? Natural Disasters? Weather? Feelings, Behaviours and Attitudes of others? Do you realize majority of life problems we face is because we try to control things we really cannot control? We are constantly trying to control things and people we have no ability to do so. For example we are trying so hard to avoid death, but we really can't. Instead if we accept that it's not something we can't control, the moment we accept it – it takes away the fear of death. Same goes to aging, sickness and other things. As humans we have no control over these. We cannot go beyond these and this is how the world operates. We may think as humans we have the power and the ability to do everything, but in reality we don't. Understanding this and accepting this will give you peace. Instead of avoiding death, let's try to live life with joy and peace in this moment. Instead of avoiding aging, let's try to live gracefully through aging. Instead of trying not to catch a disease, let's try to maintain good health as best as possible. Instead of trying to control other people's feelings, let's try to accept those. Instead of trying to get someone to love and like us, lets love and like ourselves so that we can love and like others freely. Instead of trying to control other people's behaviours, let's try to control ours. Regardless who we are, we only have 24 hours per day. No one can extend it. No one gets an extra second. We cannot beg, borrow or steal time. What is gone is gone. So what are you doing with your 24 hours? All we can do is use the time in our hands wisely. **Why deplete our limited energy trying to do things we really cannot?**

Trying to control things we cannot control

Now step back and think further, aren't we trying to control the very same things that we really cannot control? Isn't this the reason why we are always stressed? Anxious? Fearful? The Curtain Call will come for everyone; it's not something we can avoid. Anyone who is born will die. We cannot run away from death. We cannot hide. We can't tell when but we will face death.

That is the only thing that is certain in this life. Some live for long and some for short – some do all the things that is right and by the book but still fall critically ill and go through long suffering before death. Yet some live so recklessly and do all the so called bad things and then experience a very peaceful death. How do you really justify these things? And is it needed? We cannot expect to understand every little thing about this world. We also don't need to. There will always be things we don't understand and we have to ask ourselves, how important is it for me to know this? We have to understand and accept our limitations as humans and where we stand in our world. There is a place for us, and there is a place for the birds, animals, trees, mountains, rivers, lakes, sea, sky, sun, moon and the stars too. As children we understood this and accepted this reality without doubt, but as we become adults we are not very open to this reality. We are not the world; we are only a very small part of the world. This world is much bigger than us.

As you can see in this phase we have consciously taken the time to look at ourselves in detail. We are the product of our own lives; in fact we are the only product of our lives. Before we live, play or perform with our product we need to know and understand our product well. He tells me majority of us don't take the time to do that. We take our product out to the market way too early without really getting to know us. What we need to live, play, and perform is all inside of us. Everything is provided for us, including the talents, gifts, tools, equipment and also the instructions, but to find that we need to take that inner journey. Imagine buying a new car. With a new car comes a detailed instruction manual. But it's never given to your hand or placed on the driver's seat, but it is inside the cubby hole (the glove compartment) of the car. One must open the cubby hole and take it out. How many of us, ever take the time to read the manual? Most of us assume we know everything in there, but when we get stuck with something – still we don't bother to read the instruction manual. We prefer to ask people around. How many times have we been misguided or misdirected when asking others? But yet, we still do this again and again. Because we are conditioned to behave this way. Same way, we do this with our own lives. This is why, in this phase the journey is inwards, because we have to go inside to find our true self. And this is what we did. I hope now you have a better understanding of yourself. We looked at our Internal Operating System, our Gifts and Talents, our Weaknesses and Barriers, our 4 Corner-Pillars of our Life Stage, our Role Models and our Ideal Life. We realise that we may also have to live without something or someone we really want or need. Because it is all part of the plan. We also looked at our limitations as humans. Sometimes, we forget or overlook we have limitations as humans. We tend to think that we can control anything and everything. We now, clearly know that we can't. Take time to reflect on what you discovered about your TRUE self.

Living with Gratitude

Sure, we may not always get what we want, but most of the time we have everything we need. He tells me that we are given what we need, not necessarily everything we want. Let's live with gratitude and be thankful for the things we have and things that are working well in our lives. It can be different things for different people. Take time to value and appreciate what you already have that is good in your life. You may want to make a list if that helps.

Who are you? Who are you really?

Once you have a clear idea of who you are then we can move to discovering our Source. Who is your Source?

Are you the Smart Phone or are you the Source of Energy that energises the Smart Phone. My understanding through completing this process is I am only the Smart Phone. As the Smart Phone, my energy is limited. I have to be charged regularly, if not daily.

Phase Two

Taking you on an Upward Journey to connect you with your Source/Creator

Discover Your Source

I will start with asking you a question:

Do you believe in a power greater than yourself?

Who is your Creator? Your Source? Your Inventor? Your Master? Your Artist? Your Potter? Your Designer? Your Architect?

Let me ask you this question in another way.

If you were that Coffee Cup we talked about in Phase One, who created you?

Depending upon what is fed into your system and what you currently believe about your existence, your answer could be connected to a religious or spiritual path, or not; and it is not important. What is important here is your answer to this question. Most will have an answer or have an idea. It may not be clear as black or white at this time. It is okay if your answer is grey. And if that is where you are then it is where you are and let's accept it.

Let me explain - let us look at a Smart Phone. The phone is loaded with fantastic apps that perform all sorts of wonderful tasks for you. But in order for your phone to work you need to have energy – yes, that is electrical current or power. Without power your phone is of no use, regardless what wonderful apps you have installed. Therefore, you need to plug it in on a regular basis to fill it with power – likely to a wall socket that provides you with power. So imagine if you were this Smart Phone who gives you power? Or what gives you power? Who do you plug in to? Somebody or something has to give you energy, as we need energy to run our lives — who provides that to you? Take some time to reflect on this question.

For some of you, the answer to this very important question may come from an established religious or spiritual path, and you may identify this Source/Creator as - God, Lord, Almighty, Higher Power, Buddha, Jesus, Allah, Krishna, Shiv, Universe, Baba, Master Teacher, Holy Trinity, Mother God, Father God, Jehovah, Yeshua, Holy Spirit, Divine Being, Yahweh, Universe, Mohammad, Abraham, Supreme Being or Spirit or any other name. Whatever name you call it is okay, what is important is that you have established a connection to your Source and you identify a power greater than you. If you are the Smart Phone, then the Wall Socket will be your Source/Creator.

Discover you Path to the Source

My Source tells me that just as there are several names to Source, there are several paths to the Source. This is how he explains it and this makes perfect sense to me. Imagine the Top of a Mountain as the HOME of your Source. Now there could be several paths to the Mountain Top. These paths to that mountain top can be different religions, yes -different religions that exist in the world today such as Christianity, Islam, Buddhism, Hinduism, Judaism, Zen, etc. Some are more popular and well known established paths and some lesser known. Some paths may show on GPS and some may not but what matters is that they all lead to the Mountain Top. On certain paths there may be more followers, but just because there are more followers this does not mean that it is the only correct path. Please keep this in mind. Over time, some of these paths may have established certain customs, rituals and routines. Therefore, a person who is following a particular path may be subjected to these customs, rituals and routines. The most important thing to consider is do you have a connection with your Source, while walking on this path? This is the most important aspect of your journey, having that one-on-one connection with your Source. If you have established that connection it is great - then proceed. If you have not, then you are not on the right path at this time of your life. Please understand, for most of us, this path is assigned at birth by others, without our permission. So many of us may walk on these paths as sleepwalkers. We may not feel the connection to Source but just continue to walk, following all the customs, rituals and routines. Who are we trying to please? Take time to reflect on your journey between YOU and your Source. **This is YOUR life and this about YOUR journey.** Finding your Source and the connection is extremely important for your life. It's your Source that has the plan to your

True Purpose in life. This can be revealed only by your Source and no one else.

As he says, if your path works for you, stay on your path. What does it mean when he says work for you? Have you established a strong one-on-one connection with your Source? Are you your most authentic version walking on this path? Are you at peace walking on this path? Are you represented well walking on this chosen path? If you say "yes" stay. If not look around, take time to explore and find a path that suits you. I am not here to tell you which path is better. This is not my place to say so. What is good for you is your own choice. The path I was admitted at birth, after some years did not give me peace or satisfaction. Today this path is heavily taken over by traditions, customs, routines and rituals. Unfortunately, I cannot feel the connection to my Source by following this path. I no longer could pretend I was happy. More so, I was disturbed and felt uncomfortable. Following that path was hindering my progress. I simply could not connect to my Source by following those routines and rituals. Sometimes I engaged in them to show the world that I belonged to that path just to please the people around me. I may have made others happy but I was unhappy myself and I was also dishonest to myself. Blindly following those routines and rituals did not make any sense to me. This path was once a pure path – intuitively I know this, but over time this has become corrupted; the issue is not the Source who led it, the issue is the people who followed it over time; they did not take the responsibility and care it needed to protect the purity of the path. Just like any old road, over time and use, the road gets damaged, and if people who use the road don't take care to repair the damages the road becomes unsafe for its travellers.

Please pay attention and reflect here. This is happening to many established paths at this current time. These were paths once that safely led its followers to the mountain top in the past, but with time many of these paths have broken down and have become unsafe to travel. Beware, some paths will take you in circles around the mountain but not take you to the top. If you are in a path like this, what should you do? Should you find another path that is suitable for you? Should you stay there hoping the path gets cleared? Knowing that you are not heading anywhere, should you remain there to please others or to prove your loyalty? These questions are for you to answer.

How to connect with your Source

So you have identified your Source and the Path to walk on, now how do you connect to your Source? Different people engage in different activities, or rituals or practices that will help build this connection, please note this can be different things to different people; these can be attending church, temple, mosque, synagogue, gurudhwar, mandir, engaging in traditional prayer, meditation, reading scripture or specific guide books such as - the Bible, the Quran, the Thripitaka, the Bhagavat Gita, Torah, Talmud, etc., chanting mantras, being part of a religious/spiritual group, practicing/observing certain rituals, being still, attending events at different religious institutions, the list goes on. **Do what works for you. This is about you and creating your one-on-one connection with your Source. This is not about what others think of you.** Allow yourself to feel this connection within yourself.

Let me give you an example, currently I use an iPad and also an LG smart phone. They are both great machines with some fantastic apps. However, they both have to be connected differently to charge with power. I cannot use the same adaptor for iPad and LG. They also have two completely different operating systems – iOS and

Android - although same apps such as Facebook or Messenger can be run on either machine. Isn't it the same for us humans? I hope this makes sense. Find your own unique method or methods to connect with your Source.

Personal Relationship with your Source

I call my Source "God" – and I affectionately I call him "Boo. It is something that came to my mind to call him and I do that with utmost love and respect. When it comes to love and respect, he is at the very top for me. But some may feel offended that I call God – Boo because it is not a traditional term. So out of curiosity, I looked it up in the dictionary and the English meaning shows as "said suddenly to surprise someone" or "utterance of "boo" to show disapproval or contempt". Even after knowing this, I still felt strongly to call him "Boo" so I continued to search further. I found that the French meaning is "someone you love or adore" - I was truly joyful to know this because this is exactly what it means to me to call him "Boo" and this is something that comes from my heart. I understand I don't have to justify this to anyone, and God is my Boo.

When I am connected to God he provides me with everything I need to live my life: guidance, wisdom, power, strength, love etc. I do not need to go to any special place to connect to him. I do not attend temple or church or any other religious place of worship. I do not engage in any traditional methods to connect with him. I do not know scripture or mantras. Prayer to me is simply talking to him, yes, in simple and plain language. Meditation is listening to him talk. When I am still, and aligned with him, I can hear his voice - it's a sense of voice in my mind. I am able to connect directly with him when I am engaged in things, activities and projects that I love to do; things that comes straight from my heart, things that I am passionate about - such as listening to my favourite music, when I am interacting with children or animals or when I am in nature, or if I am creating something from my heart, a piece of art, writing, developing curriculum, teaching, coaching, counselling or facilitating, playing music, dancing, etc. I am able to see my Source in everyday life – I am able to connect and see his hand in the creation of a butterfly or a beautiful flower in the wilderness, in a feather of a bird, in dew drops and in rain and the smiles and eyes of babies, – in nature, in all things positive and beautiful. When I am engaged in these, I am living consciously in the moment. And it is in this moment my Source is most vibrant and alive. I am able to hear from him, feel him and sense him. It's a beautiful feeling, a deep felt love, compassion and kindness that I have never received from any human. I feel accepted and loved and valued for who I am, with all my flaws and weaknesses. Yet in this moment I feel I am complete and I am good enough even though I know that I have flaws. In this moment I know I can do anything with my Source beside me. And he reminds me that this is available for everybody.

I felt my connection when I was very young. As young as 3 or 4 years old. I heard his voice — it was a sense of a voice which I heard in my mind. So I didn't know what to make out of it, I wasn't scared of the voice but I did not want to talk about it with others. But as I grew older this voice and sense of his presence got very strong and I started to hear from him very clearly. I still didn't follow his guidance but I clearly heard it on a regular basis. It was most prominent when I was meditating. From a very young age I had the habit of meditating, it is not something someone taught me. In 1995, after my father's departure he took over and became my constant guide and has been my constant companion since then.

He led me through some very difficult and dark times of my life. At times, when I had absolutely no one beside me, he was always there.

Today I have a strong one-on-one relationship with my Source; it came with faith, trust and belief. It wasn't easy at the beginning – No, it was not a cakewalk – it was just like any other relationship but practice made it strong. He is that "Wall Socket" of energy I plug into. I need to plug into him daily not just once but several times. When I do plug into him I have access to vast wisdom. It is a truly amazing and humbling experience. I cannot quite explain it in words but the vibrations are felt in my body. For this to happen I have to stay still, and make my connection strong with him; with my body, mind and soul directly aligned with Source in the present moment. The wisdom I am sharing with you is not mine; this wisdom is not taught to me by my parents, schools or any of the institutions I have attended. He teaches me the most amazing things about life, his teaching is very simple and clear and he uses simple, everyday language to teach me – he uses real life examples when teaching. He encourages me to learn from being present in the moment and paying attention to my surroundings; people, nature, animals and basically life. He is the BEST TEACHER - I have ever met – loving, patient, kind, respectful and also fun. This wisdom I am sharing with you is downloaded to me when I plug into my Source. He tells me that this is accessible to all – yes, to each and every one of you – this has absolutely nothing to do with belonging to a religion, or attending a particular religious institution or practicing any routines or rituals. What I do has no-name, but it works for me. I strongly believe it's possible for you too if you wish to try. All you do is to connect with your Source through these unconventional, no-name but heart-felt methods. You are not harming yourself or anyone else with what you do. You can do this in your own time, in your own preferred environment. It is there, if you wish to experience.

I strongly encourage you to engage in activities you love and like on a regular basis. Stay connected to who you truly are. That is why we spent a lot of time to cleanse your cup in the first phase. It is important you did that and I hope you took the time to complete all assignments. Only after you complete that phase you will realize who you truly are. Consciously become more and more of this person. Bring your true authentic self into surface. When you consciously do this you will start to feel connected to your Source. Please know that this is open to all, regardless of which religion or faith group you represent. As you develop a stronger connection you will start to receive information and messages from your Source. It will come to you in your own unique method. So please pay attention. If at the beginning the connection is not strong don't get discouraged, please be patient and stay with it. Give it some time.

Receiving Information from your Source

Pay attention to how you receive messages from your Source. You may identify your Source as living energy – it is around you and it will certainly communicate with you if you are open to communicating. This is why you need to stay connected so that you can keep the communication lines open – through this you will get the necessary information and messages. Each individual is unique and therefore how you receive information is also unique. Some may clearly be able to identify this energy as male or female. I identify this as male energy. Some of you may distinctively hear his voice, or feel his presence, see images or even exposed to different tastes and smells. I hear, feel and sense.

These are my strong receiving modes. For me, hearing is subjective, so as the sensing and feeling – this means it comes from my body and not from outside. In my minds ear – I hear his voice; I also experience a unique sense of feeling and extra ordinary sensing in my body. For some this may be objective, meaning you may experience this coming outside of your own body. I also receive information coming as a deep sense of knowing. I know that I know - that I know, but I do not know how I know. I combine all these methods to gather his messages. Each person has this ability, so please pay attention and find your own unique method. It is there, but it is yours to discover.

Walking on the "Road less Travelled"

Today, I am led on a path that has no name. But it is a road less travelled. Yes, not many people are on this path. But I am walking on this path with my Source. This path suits me well at this time. Upon completing Phase One, I have cleared my Coffee Cup and I am free from clutter. I don't hold on to any labels. I only see myself as human. I have freed myself from traditions, cultural habits, rules, values, beliefs that no longer serve me. So I travel free and light on this path. I am now more connected to my Source, and I have a stronger one-on-one relationship with my Source. While walking on this path, I make time to connect with him on a daily basis. I talk to him, listen to him and chat with him in plain simple language. Yes just simple plain English. My Source is living energy – its real and it's alive. He is with me at all times. I can include him in my life or exclude him, I realize it's a choice I have. He does not intrude. He does impose. But, today I have made the choice to include him because my life is marvellously better with him. I no longer belong to any established religion. Please note, I do respect followers of all religions. I am not here to promote or put down any religion. I could not tell you which is better or which is not. I am very clearly instructed not to make that choice for you. I am only asked to assist you to find your path. I am happy with my chosen path. I know I am on the right path because I see progress every single day. I am more happier and peaceful now than ever before, I feel my life is meaningful and rewarding.

In the past, I used to give this place I give my Source - to different people in my life. But, now I realize that people in general have limitations – because they are human. They have limited knowledge, limited abilities, limited capabilities, limited access, limited love and limited tolerance. They change with the situation or the environment. All humans change over period of time, they are not capable of providing another unconditional, love, support etc. All humans experience light and dark in their lives. They cannot remain constant at all times. A human who has given you love for many years can change instantly. It is the nature of being human. This is a reality of life I discovered on my own. I change and others change too. I have not remained constant through my journey. My love, support, appreciation for others have also changed over time. I am certainly not knowledgeable in all areas and all aspects of life. The power, wisdom, tolerance, knowledge and love I hold is very much limited. Let me explain, this is like instead of connecting to the Wall Socket for power, you connect to a Battery Pack. The battery pack can only power you for a limited time. It cannot give you constant energy. Eventually, battery pack also has to be charged. This is the same when we rely on other human beings for power. It's temporary. It's sometimes good for a short period of time but it is not a permanent solution.

Unlimited and FREE access

I discovered my Source has unlimited knowledge, abilities, capabilities, access, love and tolerance and my Source is better equipped to serve me and provide the life energy I need 24x7x365. I can always access him day or night, and I am not limited to any communication equipment or mode of transportation. I can connect anywhere, anytime and costs no money to do that. Best part is it's FREE and provides life-time service. Today, I live a life that is very much depended on my Source — but I have freed myself to a large extend on depending on other people. This does not mean that I don't need people anymore. I do not isolate myself from others. But my relationships are becoming more freeing. I am learning to give without expecting anything in return. It is not easy because I am conditioned to expect things in return. But I am learning to unlearn. I am simply able to be in a relationship because I want to. Not because I want something from someone. In the past, I have taken roles and relationships in life simply because I depended so much on others. I hope you will get to experience this for yourself. And that is exactly what he wants for you and from you.

Receiving your Blueprint

Once you start a solid connection with your Source, your Source will start to show you the blueprint to your own unique life. It will happen step by step as you develop faith, trust and belief in your Source. In my own experience, you will not be given the whole plan at once. One little baby step is how it happened to me. It is a walk of faith, trust and belief with your Source. You are here for a purpose and a reason. It is important we understand and live life on purpose. It is our responsibility and obligation to do so. You are here for a reason. You were created with a specific reason, each and every one of us were created for a special purpose. In order for this world to balance we must act on our purpose. This world is his Master Plan. However, many of us, once we get here forget why we came here and start to pursue purposes of our own. People have forgotten the real purpose of life. People have forgotten we are only here for a very short time and we come with nothing and go with nothing – but yet, while we are here – we are overly obsessed about accumulating material wealth. We seem to think if we try harder, or work harder we could avoid death. But we must realize we cannot. Most of our purposes are around our own selves or own little families. But these purposes are selfishly formed with our limited vision. Many of us are unable to see the bigger picture. Hence this is why this concept is introduced to you now. The present world has gone out of balance and in a crisis situation. Disasters are happening all over the world. The world is in some kind of darkness. We have to correct this situation soon. And for that he needs to prepare people who will take up those positions. Those of you who are assigned you will know this. This book is written specifically for YOU.

Your Source – Your Navigator

Your Source is the best GPS in the world. Your Source will lead you but will also give you clear directions and will tell you if you need to turn right, left or go straight or even make a U turn. I was instructed to make a U turn and I did. Yes, I was going in a completely different direction and he asked me to turn around. It is your Source who will lift you towards positivity in life. In our world of duality, there is an upward pull and also a downward pull. Notice this. If you make your Source your Anchor in your life it will keep you stable even in times of difficulty and constantly guide you to travel upwards.

Niroma De Zoysa

Contribute or Contaminate?

Do you realize at any given time, as a human you have a choice to contribute or to contaminate? Yes you do, with your thoughts, with your words and actions – you can contribute to the betterment of yourself and world or do the opposite! Pretty powerful isn't it that we have this ability? Now which side would you pick? It is your choice! Should you decide you want to travel upwards, universe will support you. Should you decide you want to travel downwards, again universe will support you. Pretty amazing isn't it? Take time to think and reflect. For an example, take your ability to sing - that could be a gift you received from your Source. Now in utilizing this gift, you can decide to contribute to the society by singing beautiful, meaningful, melodious songs; music is healing when you use it appropriately with the correct sound vibrations. But you can also contaminate the society if you use it as improper music vibrations – the music becomes toxic and disturbing. Think about it, the same seven notes can be presented to heal or destroy – it can pull up or push down. Which side would you choose? It is your choice! Are you going to be a contributor or a contaminator? It is your choice. You can do this with anything – even a gift you have received. Think and reflect.

Life Purpose

Today, I have a very clear idea of my life purpose. It is very different from the dream I had of my own. My dream was to be a submissive wife to a powerful, handsome man. For the life of me, I can't understand why submissive! I wanted to do everything to make my husband shine and become his shadow. I also wanted to have six baby boys and two german shepherd dogs. I wanted to live in a big beautiful house overlooking a lake with a large lawn. I wanted to be a housewife hosting beautiful tea parties. Yes, my dream was very specific, very detailed, I crafted it for myself since I was sixteen years old. That was what I wanted and what I worked for. But upon connecting with my Source, I got to know his plan for me. He revealed his plan to me very slowly, not all the steps came at once. It came one step at a time, and he had to prepare me to get to this stage to receive the complete plan. Journey started 23 years ago, but 20 years ago I would not be able to comprehend the plan he had for me if he fully revealed it to me, not 15 years ago, not 10 years ago, and not even 5 years ago. I realize looking back why my own sweet plan never worked for me. It was not designed that way by the Master Planner. Today I have a very clear idea of my life purpose. I realize now I wasn't called to play house, wife or mother. But I was created for something else. Today, I agree and I understand why I need to do what I am called for. There is a need and it is for the betterment of this world. Sure, there is sadness in me for not been able to achieve my own dream, but when I look at the overall bigger picture – I totally understand why I need to do what I need to do. And now, I am in full agreement to fulfill this purpose. Writing this book for him has been a major part of my assigned life purpose. If we all did what we came here to do, our world will be heaven on earth. It is designed that way. There is abundance. There is enough for everyone. The issue is we are not doing what we came here to do. We have terribly messed things up, if we continue we will completely destroy this beautiful earth. He knows this and he sees this and you the reader will see this too. He also knows, not everyone will embrace this concept at this time. But he tells me some will do and they need to take the lead to take the necessary action. This concept is for them. You will understand this concept clearly because it is in you to understand it. Are you one of them?

May this book reach those people that he is seeking. May you be the person that he is seeking.

Phase Three
Taking you on an Outward Journey to connect you with the outside world

This phase is about all your external relationships - this is about creating and maintaining positive, rewarding relationships with others in your life. We as humans were created to live with others; we were not created to live in isolation. So creating and maintaining harmonious, productive and pleasant relationships are important. This is also about understanding the different roles you play, choosing which roles to continue to play and evaluating its importance, and meaning in your present life.

Building and maintaining relationships usually becomes the top priority in many of our lives. This is also where we usually spend most of our time, energy and resources - forming and maintaining external relationships. Habitually, we give a lot of importance to forming and maintaining relationships with others in our everyday lives. It starts with our birth as babies and continues - and it cannot be avoided. Often times we spend more time in building relationships with others than we give time to ourselves or to our Source. He tells me this is where we have gone wrong. He tells me that relationships with others are important but never more important than the relationship we have with ourselves and also with our Source. This may be a new way of thinking for many of us. It certainly was for me. Many of us have never heard of building a relationship with ourselves. For some it may sound crazy or silly or even purely selfish. This I now certainly see as a paradigm shift! So with this new concept – this is the last phase. Isn't this an interesting shift? Now I understand this was for a very good reason. And it makes perfect sense to me why this phase needs to be the last. I hope it does to you too.

Once you know more about yourself all your external relationships will fall in to place. You will know what is important and what is not in your life. You will understand and know the real meaning of your external relationships and why you really need to form relationships with others.

Let's look at your most important external relationships – your significant other – spouse or lover, your children, your immediate family – your parents and siblings, your relatives, co-workers, customers, neighbours, and all other type of associates – all these relationships play an important role in your life. Some of them can certainly be a blessing to you; their association will help to strengthen your wellbeing and empower you and help you become your very best self. Then there are relationships that could be toxic and unhealthy. They can really put you down and hinder your progress. Therefore, we must be mindful in choosing these relationships. How much time and energy is spent on these relationships is something you need to take into consideration. Again carefully evaluate – are these relationships helping you to become your BEST? Or, are they hindering your progress? If they are hindering your progress in any way, should you continue to maintain those relationships? Some relationships can be purely abusive – physically, emotionally, financially, sexually or any other way; if they are toxic or abusive should you hold on to those?

Now that you have new wisdom and awareness should you continue to maintain relationships with people who are toxic or bring harm to you? There questions are yours to answer.

With the new wisdom and awareness I have received, here is what I understood about my relationships. I believe people cross my path for a reason and there is a lesson I need to learn with each crossing. These people come as parents, siblings, relatives, friends, associates, etc. Every person I cross paths with comes with an important lesson. Every encounter is for a reason and for my higher good and it is only because I need to learn that lesson to enhance my journey and purpose in life. They all teach me something, sometimes the lesson is positive, pleasant and joyful and other times, the lesson is negative, unpleasant and sorrowful. But they are both equally valuable to my journey. They are all important life lessons. They all come to show me and confirm the duality of life which is common to all humans; the light and dark side of life; this is life – life is both dark and light. Birth and death, night and day, sun and moon, happiness and sadness, joy and sorrow, success and failure and the list goes on. He tells me to consider each person I cross paths as a teacher, and consider each encounter as a lesson. He tells me to value each teacher and learn the lesson he/she is teaching me. Isn't this phenomenal? I am now learning to look at life this way.

Some will come to show you love, joy, kindness, caring, truth, honesty – then there are some who come to show us anger, hatred, sorrow, heartache – usually we dislike the latter and are more open to receiving the former – but, in a balanced world both are important. How would we know light without dark? How would we know day without night? How would we know success without failure? Makes perfect sense, doesn't it?

The most valuable lessons are taught to us by members of our closest circles - such as our parents, siblings, spouse and children. These are the immediate members of our family. Sometimes the lessons are positive, sometimes they are not. Habitually, we expect them to be positive and pleasant; we want every parent to be loving, caring, protective and nurturing. But it does not always happen like that. Same with every lover or spouse we expect unconditional love, sweet romance, intimacy, understanding, support and partnership but that too does not always happen like that. How do you justify this? Why isn't every parent loving and nurturing to their children? Why isn't every spouse loving and understanding? I am sure you will have an opinion about this. So this is mine. This is where I believe that the ultimate plan of my life is not really mine, but it is the plan of my Source/Creator. He is the real Plan Maker. This I only understood after connecting to him on Phase two. With the solid connection I have formed I have come to believe that he is the Plan Maker of my life and not me. The Director of my "Life" is not I but my Source. I am the actor. I act as per the script I am provided with. But when I work closely with the director, I get to have a good understanding of my script; I begin to understand why the script is directed in a certain way because of the expected outcome of the play. This is deep. Does this make sense to you? Because of this realization, I can say that all is well and all was well with all the relationships I had in the past, even though some of them were very bitter, painful and hard. I do understand why they had to be, and why some didn't work out as I planned.

The bottom line here is, all we can aspire is to - is to be a skilled actor in life. We play and perform as per the script. Every actor is good – regardless of the role we play as each actor is a unique creation of the Creator, even the one who plays villain; at the end of the play we are all good and we are friends. But we have to wait until the "Curtain Call" to experience this. We must remember that we shake hands and hug only after the "Curtain Call" and not before! Until then we have to act our part. Isn't this phenomenal? If only we really could get this in our heads! I believe our hearts already know this truth. I don't think I need to inject this to you, I think deep down you know this to be true.

Same goes to parents, spouse, friends and all other relationships too. So let us stay objective and learn the lesson. What are they teaching you? When a relationship is not going well I believe we can make reasonable efforts to make things right and continue the relationship; but if it's continually harming you physically, emotionally or spiritually I believe we must cultivate enough love and respect for ourselves and move away. Making this decision and taking the action is also a lesson we need to learn. This was a huge lesson in my life as I held on to some very toxic relationships. It took a very long time for me to learn these lessons. These lessons came from close circle relationships. People I expected to protect me - harmed me. People I expected to love me did not love me back. People I expected to nurture me - abandoned me. My Source signalled me numerous times to remove myself and move on but I still held on because I felt guilt and thought I didn't have the right to free myself because of the close ties attached. I went back and forth with some of these relationships for decades. I suffered immensely. My Source finally had to intervene to close some doors for me. I wasn't strong enough to close some of them on my own. Some endings were painful. But with these lessons he taught me self-love, self-respect and self-protection. He also showed me to forgive them completely for any harm they did to me before I let them go. So finally when I let them go, I was able to let them go completely without any strings attached. He showed me why I have to let them go, because they are hindering my progress. Their part in my life was over. My next stage did not include them. It was a truly liberating experience. This is huge, take time to think and reflect.

Sometimes, we hold on to pain, neglect, abuse and disrespect simply because it is inflicted by a close family member or a dear friend. Often times, these lessons are taught to us by the very same people we look up to or people we love and respect. We expect love, respect, support, care, understanding but what they are showing is just the opposite of what we expect – hate, disrespect, abuse, neglect etc. It is extremely disappointing and painful but he tells me that we need to stand aside and look at things objectively. That is the role they are playing in our lives and we must stop expecting anything else. As much as it's difficult we must accept that and learn the lesson. After we learn the lesson then it's time to move on. Many of us hold on to the relationship long after the lesson is learnt. Some of us during this time destroy ourselves. I certainly did it myself. At times, I did not have the courage and confidence to move forward even though I received the signal from my Source. I still expected human support. I wanted someone to save me. But the people I expected to support did not support me. Now, when I look back – this too was a lesson for me to learn – not to rely on human support. There are times in life, we have to go without. I believe this was a lesson where I had to learn that "I am enough". And it was a huge and powerful lesson for me. Beautiful isn't it?

In the past, I gave my relationships top priority. I wanted all people around me to love me and like me. My relationships were based on constantly getting myself filled. I was like an empty bucket; I depended on them to fill me with love, self-worth, appreciation, validation and approval. In order to earn that I thought I had to please them constantly, and this meant for me to constantly agree with them or show support to them even though at times I did not want to. In behaving this way now I realize I was really dishonest to myself. I chose to do things that I did not like. I was in places I did not want to be. I was involved in projects and activities I did not really want to get involved. I said "yes" to things when deep down I wanted to say "no" but didn't know any other way. My life was filled with people, activities, events and projects that meant nothing to me. My agenda was full. I was super busy living a life that did not fulfill me. I was constantly miserable and exhausted. I didn't feel joy; I didn't feel meaningful or productive with what I was doing. It drained me and made me sick physically and emotionally. I felt angry and resentful at times. I didn't think my life had any authenticity. I felt trapped and suffocated in those relationships.

But with the connection of Source in my life, my life has changed. My cup is cleansed and my path has changed. I have a better sense of who I am today and where I am going. Today I nurture genuine, loving relationships – nurturing relationships are still very important. However, my intention has changed considerably. I am not a people pleaser anymore. I truly and genuinely care for the people I associate. All people who are in my immediate circle are people who love and accept me for who I am, and I do the same for them too. There is not a huge number that is in my inner circle, but I now go with quality over quantity and I am very happy with my relationships. They give me joy and peace. I no longer give prominence to a title or so-called blood or family connections; I look at the quality of the relationship. I have cultivated enough self-love, and my cup is filling with love that comes from within. I am able to quickly say NO to abusive relationships. I live with mindfulness and when I see unwanted trouble coming my way, I cross the road – or I give myself the permission to run. I know that I no longer have to go head-on, I know better now; I have the right to protect myself. Prior to mastering this concept, I was very eager to serve people. I was very quick with my rescue operations. I volunteered myself to rescue people and often got myself injured through the process. I did not consider my own safety that is because I did not love or care for myself. I jumped in to rescue others but some were not interested in getting recued. They were happy in their chosen tunnels. They were settled there and had no plans to get out. But by over extending my hand to rescue others who really did not want to, some dragged me in to their misery tunnel. It was hard to get out. And on such times it was my Source who pulled me up to the light. I realize now this is what people pleasers do to themselves. But strangely, upon connecting to my Source, I see myself limiting my rescue operations. I now wait for his direction to get involved with my rescue operations. I do not jump in without considering my safety anymore. And when I jump in I do it because I am asked to do so by my Source and I go with back up support. I also have my safety clothing on and I am now better equipped. I hope this makes sense to you.

I still need other people in my life. I enjoy interacting and forming relationships with others. But I am no longer heavily dependent on others. I have a clearer understanding of who I am now, and understand others much better. Prior to this knowledge I very much depended on others for many things. But I no longer do that. I know who gives me what. I am now freer with my relationships. I am able to give without many expectations. I would not say that I don't have any expectations yet, but with time I want to work on this.

I also understand that I have the right to choose my life roles, and choose them wisely. I no longer hold on to toxic relationships be it with family, friends or associates. When people show me their true colours, I accept them. I no longer try to whitewash anyone. Every now and then, I come across people who totally surprise me with their behaviours. Some only take and never stay long enough to give. Some serve me bitterness, hurt and pain even when I serve them love, kindness, support and understanding; some friendships are just simply one sided. As much as it brings heartache, I am learning to see these as essential lessons. I welcome positive, pleasant, productive relationships that are good for me. Anything and anyone that is no longer serving my best interests I let go with much ease. With these choices, I am able to form and maintain genuine relationships in my life.

Conclusion

I want to share with you the following in my conclusion.

My life has become much peaceful, rewarding and meaningful upon adapting to this life concept. I am much happier and feel at peace with my life. This concept is put together based on the wisdom I received from my Source. What I love most is my life has become very simple and clutter free! Today, I know who I am, and I am very content and at ease with who I am. I have also developed a very strong connection with my Source. I am very clear with my life path and I am taking steps to fulfill my life purpose before I depart this world. It is also my desire to do so.

This concept is focussed on myself and my inner world, and how I look at the outer world; this is not about changing others or the world. It helped me to discover who I am and my true self and my true assets. My outer world and people around still remains same, but how I look at it has changed and it makes a huge difference. Problems, issues and concerns are still there, I cannot control them or eliminate them but I am starting to look at them in a different way – in new light. The world may be dark and chaotic but I realize I do not have to go with it; I can still remain calm and retain my peace and serenity within myself. This concept helped me to prioritize my life and my path – clarified what I need to carry within myself for me to continue with the rest of my journey here on earth and live my life with purpose and meaning.

I have eliminated many things that no longer serve me. I am no longer attached to unnecessary labels that do not serve me well. I refrain from holding on to labels that separates me from other humans. I no longer see its importance in my chosen journey. I see myself as a human and this world as my classroom. Clearing my cup was not easy. Yes, it was a very tedious process but it was well worth it. What is inside my cup are things I have chosen myself with much thought and reflection. I am responsible and accountable for all the things I carry and hold in my cup. There isn't anything in there that I don't want. The values and beliefs I hold are things I still want and value. My Life Stage is reconstructed. It is not the same stage I used to perform on. The 4 Corner-Pillars have considerably thinned down in size. My life is becoming lot simpler. I am also now very protective of my cup. I keep my lid closed most of the time – this means I have established personal boundaries. I do not allow others to throw litter in to my cup.

I now have a very good understanding of what my Source has gifted me. I value and appreciate all the gifts and talents I have received, they are my permanent assets, no one can take them away from me. I am very proud to own my gifts and talents and I am utilizing them all to fulfill my life purpose. All those gifts and talents are essential to fulfilling my life purpose. I am beginning to feel at peace with my life. All is well and perhaps for the first time I understand what this means. I know I am not perfect but I feel complete. I no longer feel the need to look outside of myself to feel complete. I also have a clear understanding of my weaknesses and barriers and the areas I need to continue to work on. There are many things in this world I don't know of, certain things I am interested in learning and certain other things I am not interested in knowing. I am at peace with the knowing and unknowing and I understand it is not possible for me to know everything and there is also no need for me to do that. I am at ease with what I know and don't know.

I understand my inner world much clearly now. I know I am much more than my physical body; I am actually multidimensional, I am a spiritual being having a human experience on earth. I know who I am and why I am like this. My life path is very much different from my childhood friends I grew up with. Today, I have chosen to walk the road less travelled. I also understand my capacity as a human. I am very clear with what I can do and also what I cannot do as a person and also as a human. I focus on what I can do and I try to do my best. There are many things I have no control of. In the past, most sorrow came from trying to control people and situations I could not control. Now, I just let them be. I understand nothing or no one lasts forever and everything changes in time - including myself.

I understand who my Source is. My Source is living energy that I can have a relationship with and connect with. And it is a beautiful and rewarding relationship that is open for all who are interested in developing. It is my choice to have a relationship with my Source. I understand the capabilities of my Source. My Source has powers and abilities that I don't have as a human. I can rely on my Source for unconditional love, wisdom, strength, knowledge, guidance, support, security, partnership, friendship and many other things - 24x7x365 – anytime, anywhere.

I also now understand my outside world more clearly - my relationships and partnerships. In the past, these controlled my life heavily. I was in relationships and partnerships simply to please others. I wanted to please others because I wanted something back from them – love, appreciation, validation, approval, etc. I have now developed enough self-confidence and I no longer look for these in others. I understand that I cannot get anyone to love me or like me. I also cannot love or like a person by force. Today, I am becoming freer with loving and accepting people. I am now able to attract meaningful, genuine, rewarding relationships in my life.

I have a better understanding of life in general now. I know life is a combination of light and dark – this duality is the reality of life. Our physical life here on earth is a journey between our birth and death. We are only here for a limited time. If we are born then we will also die and death cannot be avoided. Death does not depress me but motivates me. I know the "Curtain Call" can come anytime, and I am ready for it. I very much want to fulfill my life purpose before I depart, and while I work on fulfilling my life purpose, I want to live life with joy and peace-of-mind. I understand we are subjected to constant change. Regardless of how cautiously we try to live, we will from time to time experience the dark side of life – failure, unhappiness, sorrow, sadness, sickness, heartbreaks, disappointment, etc. It cannot be avoided. This is all part of life on earth. All I can do is to face it with the best of my ability. Each person I cross paths with comes with a valuable lesson. As the student of Life, my task is to learn the lesson from every teacher of life. Every lesson is important for my journey on earth. Although professionally I wear a hat as a teacher, in life I will always be a student.

My understanding is there are no bad people, as we are all wonderful creations of the Creator but once landed on earth people can become positively or negatively influenced. It's a choice we each make. We can choose to contaminate or contribute with our words, actions, thoughts and behaviours.

I realize what is most important is this moment. In this journey of life, we cannot go back. It is like a vehicle without a reverse gear, the vehicle can only go forward. It is only in this moment we can create our life. This is where life is. It is in this moment that life is happening. What we have in our hands is NOW. I am learning to live mindfully respecting and accepting each moment as it comes. This is new learning for me.

I now understand that the true value of self remains inside of us. We can only understand this if we take a risk to journey inside. Although it was a very tedious process, I am really glad I took the journey. I believe this is the best gift I could have given myself. Because of this, my cup is now lighter and simpler. I found that my diamond was covered with a lot of dirt and it had got chipped and cracked over these years. But, with the help of my Source I was able to wipe away the dirt. My Source also helped me to repair the damages. I am now in the process of shining it. While I do that, I also help others clean and polish their diamonds. Yes, this is what I do professionally. I am a Diamond Polisher, and my diamonds are humans. This is also my calling in life and what my Source wants me to do.

Our Earth is truly beautiful. If we all come together we can really make this world a heaven. There is beauty everywhere; in nature - in trees, in animals, in birds, in the sky, the stars, in the lakes and oceans. All we have to do is to open our eyes and look. It's here. It's around us.

And it is for all of us to enjoy. I consciously take time to appreciate the beauty that surrounds my everyday life. If I take the time to look, I know I can find beauty in my life and it's there.

I understand, if we don't live our lives as per our Source's plan, this world will go out of balance and topple very soon. It is already happening. The things that he warned me would happen many years ago have started to happen. I see it – the tsunamis, the earth quakes, wars and political disturbances, negative shifts in people's minds - it is all happening as he told me.

I am starting to understand and observe the natural patterns and rhythms of this world. Teachers are important so as students. Doctors are important so as patients. The city planner and city sweeper are both needed; they both perform very important roles in making this world a better place. One without the other is not possible. No single person is higher or lesser than another. Each person deserves equal respect and treatment. For some reason we are not respecting this life rule. We seem to think some of us are better than others. Why and how? We are living life like sleepwalkers. As humans, we have the ability and the capacity to think, reflect, question, clarify and take the correct action. He tells me we have got it wrong and we need to correct it before it's late. We are all equal as humans but we are unique in our talents, gifts abilities and skills and that is for a reason. There is no high or low in anyone's becoming.

Not everybody is meant to get married and raise a family. It is not for everybody and it is with a reason. Some will make great parents but not all. Some will raise wonderful children but not all. Some will make great husbands or wives but not all. Some have families and some don't. Some are called to walk all alone because that too is needed. We are unique human beings with unique purposes. It is created this way by the Master Planner for a specific reason. Some are appointed to take care of the animals, some for the trees, some for the stars, some for justice, some for women, some for children, some for men – there is a plan bigger than our own little plan. We must understand this. Bottom line, everybody is here for a reason. If everybody individually connected with the Source they will know and understand why they are here, and their role to play on earth at this very crucial time. We all have enough to live a successful life. There is abundance. There is enough for all. Everybody comes complete. We all come with what we need – it is inside of us. We each have our journey to walk on. No one else can do it for us. **We each have the potential to achieve self-actualization – that is to become the person we came here to be.**

My task is to spread this message to the people of the world. He prepared me for this task for a few decades. I didn't know this at the beginning but now I know. Sure, I want the whole world to understand this concept but I am specifically told not all will understand or accept or embrace this message at this time. I am told there are people who will and who can. I sincerely hope this book reaches out to every one of them who are ready to understand, accept and embrace this message at this time. It is important we do this to take on the changes that will occur for the next phase of this world – these are the people who will carry the light to guide others through the dark tunnel. We are currently going through this dark period in every part of the world, and every aspect of our lives too. More and more natural and man-made disasters are occurring around us as part of the mega cleaning up process. What is no longer serving will be removed eventually and this world will be cleansed. If people don't initiate the change then universe will do it. The shift has already begun.

Darkness may take over for a while and that too is needed. There is no need to blame or fear the darkness, but we need to strive hard and find a match to light a candle. Imagine ourselves as a candle; if we are a candle then our purpose is to light. While we give light to ourselves we can also help others light themselves. Even if we help thousand others light themselves, our light will never reduce. We need to know this and understand. There is no need to fear.

Offering this wisdom as a course helped me in the process of understanding this concept much clearly. I offered an in-house program and also an on-line program for 12 weeks each. First it helped me to put my journey of over two decades walking in this path into a workable, achievable curriculum. My professional training and education as an Adult Teacher, Trainer, Personal/Spiritual Coach, Career/Employment Counsellor and Workshop Facilitator helped me, to put this wisdom objectively into developing a practical curriculum. I did not know I would be asked to write a book on this but when the call came earlier this year it made things easier. My learning from offering the program helped me immensely to write this book in an objective manner. With both programs I explored different methods of expressive arts as a communication medium and I was extremely pleased with the outcome. I explored the use of expressive arts such as collaging, scrap booking, vision boarding, and expressing self with colors and textures in teaching this course: I also incorporated creative visualizations, positive affirmations, mindfulness, meditation, chanting, music, dance movement and nature walks as learning techniques. My future vision is to expand on this, promoting this concept through in-house and on-line programs and retreats locally and internationally.

During the time of my writing this book I was specifically instructed by my Source to refrain from discussing this with anyone. It was hard as I wanted to share this with some of my closest friends, especially with the ones who have always encouraged me to write a book. I have kept the promise and have not shared this with anyone. I was asked to complete writing this book on a certain date and I am happy to share, I made the deadline. As a recovering perfectionist, I still have a need to perfect my writing but I am asked to let go that need and forward it to the publisher. With my years of practice working with my Source, I now trust his voice and commands. I understand his directions more clearly. I also understand when he says "go" I need to drop everything and go. So here I go. I know, in all this, there are lessons for me to learn.

Here I must explain how the Source works, and how I work as a human. I was appointed by my Source to write this book. But, I wanted a few things just for myself from this project: I wanted this book to meet certain high standards and be perfect with absolutely no mistakes, and to get this book into the Bestseller List and picked up by a well-known publisher, and the list went on - I was spending my limited energy and time to make all this happen, and was feeling frantic and very much under pressure – then I heard my Source ask me **"What is in it for me? How would it help me or the work I am asking you to do? This book is not about you, it's about the work I want to do through you"** – No more questions asked, I return to my work. Yes, I got his message. This is not about me.

To my most wonderful, beautiful, like-minded friends – sorry I could not share with you about writing this book - I was under oath and I had to deliver my promise. I was strictly instructed to go alone on this project. And I know it was a test for me.

Thank you to my dear parents – Thomas De Silva and Milly Winifred Barnes Abeyawardena – De Silva – they have both departed from this world. They both had major roles in shaping my life. Thank you Dad and Mom. I also like to acknowledge each and every single person who crossed my path – they all came to teach me something, sometimes the lessons were joyful, sometimes not, but looking back I realize they always taught me what I most needed to learn at that time. Thank you to all.

Thank you to my dear Source. I hope I have delivered the message as per your request. Thank you for choosing me and using me to deliver this message on your behalf. I am truly honored. It is my sincere hope I have delivered this message as per your wish. I truly feel grateful to be alive and to be of service to my Source. I am committed to fulfilling my life purpose.

Dear readers, it is my sincere hope you benefitted from reading this book. I would love to hear your feedback - please take a few minutes to let me know. Please email me at coach_niroma@yahoo.com or check my website at www.coachniroma.com

May you discover your TRUE self and live your BEST life today, if you choose to do it - it will benefit you and also the world. It is much needed at this present time. **Stay blessed and choose to shine – light your candle first and help others to light theirs.**

Working on Your Inner Journey

I encourage you to find your own unique way to communicate with yourself as you take this inner journey. I let my feelings and emotions come to surface with writing because I feel most comfortable when I am writing – please dont worry about being perfect, my writing may not be perfect but I am comfortable with that at this stage of life, the important thing is you do something with what you have and can, with the way you know how – I am sure there are people out there who can write much better than me, more knowledgeable, more skilled, more educated, etc., etc. But this is what I can do with what I have NOW. The point is taking a risk and doing the BEST you can do - in this moment. Your BEST may not always be the BEST to others, but your BEST is what you can do. This process cleansed me and de-cluttered my inner "crap". You may choose to paint, journal, sing, compose, dance, draw, design or anything else your heart calls you to do – explore your own unique method to communicate with your inner self... Go inside, dig deep, take the journey, ask questions, think and reflect – it is all there to be discovered!

I like to share a few selected poems from my blog. This is how I communicated with my Inner Self and also my Source – while I was diving through my own inner journey to find my Diamond. I wrote in my blog from 2006 – 2011, a dark and confusing phase of my life, not many people were around me to support me but my Source, a lot of confusion and unanswered questions. I felt like that lily in mud, buried in deep mud, growing in darkness, all by myself. Many people crossed my path to teach me lessons – most were hard and some were painful – but looking back, I needed them very much to get to where I am today. They all contributed to my inner growth. Nothing was wasted!

There is more in my blog... if you wish to read... It might help you to understand what I was going through and realize you are not alone – answers are there – you just have to take the time and **ASK!**

May you find YOURSELF!

http://liveyourbestlifetoday.blogspot.com

**Discover your TRUE Self and Live
Your BEST Life TODAY!**

I am ME

I am my only wealth and asset
I am my life – my only life
I may be different from you but
I am ME….

I am sorry,
I can't be like you…
Please don't hate me for that
If I don't like what you like…
Or not think, say or do things the way you do
I may have different values, hopes and dreams
Insights and ideas, beliefs and traditions…
I may dance to a different tune
Because that is what I hear in my mind...
I may walk at a different pace
Because that is my comfort level...
I may be headed in a different direction
Because that is my destiny – meant for me...
I may be related to you
Be your husband or wife
Sister or brother
Friend or co-worker
But please don't forget
I am ME

And not you
Do not compare me to you
Because,
I am ME and not you….

I am my only wealth and asset
I am my life – my only life
This is the only time...
I can play me – in my life
This is the only time...
I can take the lead role
This is the only time...
I can shine
This is the only time...
I can be a star
By simply being me
Because I am the expert of me
This is the only time
I can put myself on the pedestal
And not feel selfish about it…
because it's me and my pedestal
Not yours or anyone elses...
but my own...

So… please let me be - the BEST me…
While you be the BEST you…

We can still be friends or family or co-workers
If you realize and accept
I am ME
And you are YOU
We can both shine
In our own unique ways…..
Without letting each other down
Or putting each other down
I am ME…

Are you, YOU? Strive to be YOU.

Thank you to YOU too

Just as much as I am thankful to all the people
Who has loved me and supported me
I am also thankful to all those who did not
I am thankful to those who told me
that I was not good enough
Because you taught me what it is to
Believe in myself and not give up my dreams

Every time you disrespected me
I learnt to respect my self even more
Every time you looked down upon me
I learnt to look up and beyond you
Every time you made me feel small
I learnt that I am actually bigger than you
Every time you told me that I was not good enough
I knew I have the ability to be even better
Every time you told me that I could not do something
I realized in fact I could do it….and do it even better

Your remarks and behaviour may
have hurt me at times
But perhaps, now that I think about it
It was for a good reason….
For every time I have experienced something bad

Even though it has been difficult and frustrating
I have always walked away being a better person
Perhaps, if not for people like you
I would have not learnt the value of self-
respect, courage, strength and perseverance
Fighting for myself and for my dreams, hopes an goals
You have challenged me to be my best
And the value of believing further
in myself and my abilities
So whether you have supported me or not
You too have made a contribution
Towards the positive growth of my life
As I continue to walk forward on my path
Whether you were on my side or not
Whether you supported me or not
Your existence in my life and my path
Has been for a good reason
So how can I not be?
Thankful to you…
Thank You!

It has taken me many years to realize, and lots of grace to admit this. Those people who have not been supportive of me are not necessarily my enemies. When I think of the great lessons

I have learnt, and the great qualities I have acquired - facing such people - I must acknowledge and give thanks to them too. I hope you try this for yourself . . . it gives so much freedom.

What Happens when somebody tells you....

What happens when somebody tells you
That you are not good enough?
Do you listen to that person?
Turn back . . . .
And give up all your hopes and dreams?

What happens to all your dreams?
Life long ambitions and aspirations?
Should you give up?
Just because,
Somebody told you – you are not good enough?

In life, it often happens
Whether you are at school, work or play
People just appear from nowhere
And tell us that we are not good enough
Or we don't belong or fit in
They tell us we have nothing to offer
No talents, skills or qualifications
Nothing worthy or valuable. . . .
Should we believe them?
Should we give in to them?
Should we give up all our hopes?
But, why?

We are who we are
And we have the right to be the best we can be
We have a right to a dream, a hope, a goal
And, we have the right to make it happen
And become successful
Just like anybody else . . .

So next time . . .
When somebody tells you that
You are not good enough
Don't turn back or walk away
Don't give up your dream or hope
Be courageous and strong
Stand still and look in the person's eye
And ask "why not?"'

"Why not?"

Many years ago, I was battling with some issues that led me to write this to myself, to give me strength. It helped me a lot and I was able to overcome some of my fears

Take this day and make something out of it....

If things are not going your way
Did you know that you could change direction?
Nothing is set or carved in stone?
Don't like what is happening with your life?
Then why don't you change it?

Change direction... if you can't move forward
Then turn to the right or left...
Or walk back if needed and find another inter-section
Do something… move... keep moving
Don't get stuck

Every day is a new day…
A new sunrise...
New hope, new dreams...
Your past is not your present
Sure there is nothing you can do about your past
Don't you wish you could go back?
And re-create everything you did wrong
And also the people who were involved in your past
Did the same thing
Said sorry, or took responsibility or did something?
But do you realize there is nothing you can do…

We have no power to change our past
or even the people involved
All we can do is to change our selves...
And to learn lessons – learn from your mistakes

Should we pay for our past mistakes forever...
Make our lives miserable...
With the dawn of a new day... God
is giving us another chance
To make things right and live our very best life...

Here we go friends...
Take this day and make something out of it...
Make it your best...
You are given another chance...

Take this day and make something out of it.

Are you running?

Stop!
Think…
What are you doing?
Where is your life flowing?
Are you just running?
Running to or running away?
Or running with the flow...
Are you living?
Or just existing?
Don't know or don't want to know...
Or
No time?
When was the last time you smiled?
When was the last time you stopped to smell the roses?
When was the last time you experienced joy?
No time?
What are you doing with your time?
Working?
For what? for whom?
Pay bills... you might say...
But what bills are you paying?
May I ask?
Are they bills you really need?

Or are they bills you think you need?
Stop! and think…
Is your money and efforts going in the wrong way...
Is it going to a drain without knowing?
I see your account is full and brimming
But yet...
Then why are you feeling so empty?
Why are you running empty?
Why are you not happy? Why are you not at peace?
Peace and happiness and tranquility
It's not for me
You might say...
But I say you are wrong...
It's also for you
Its also for all of us
But you have to find it...
It's within you

It's within your reach...
The name and status and fame and popularity
You have built or going after
I hope it will give you something back...
For you to hold on to on a dark lonely night
If the world forgets you just in case…

You are constantly running...
But my dear, where are you running?
Do you even know?
I hope...
I hope you know...
Seems like you are always in a hurry...
You don't have time for anything...
For anyone or just for you...
But you are busy...
Day and night
Weekdays and weekends...
Busy doing things...
But yet...
I don't see a smile on your face...
I don't see joy in your eyes...

So... stop and think
know where you are running to
And what you are running after
And then run on your own pace...
At your own comfort level
Don't let others push you
To run in a direction that you don't want to
At the end...
It's your run... It's your race...

Only you and you
Will meet the creator at the end...
Not me, not them
Just you!

Are you running? Where to?

Don't turn back - it's not the time...

When things are tough
Don't turn back
Muster your courage
And stay strong
And walk forward…
Yes, even if you are feeling hopeless
Empty and lonely
Just walk forward

This is the time you must listen to your inner self
Your guiding higher power
The negative voices may try to cripple you
And ask you to turn back
Give up and accept defeat
It will tell you, you are never good enough
And remind you of all your failures
Did I not tell you?
You can never be successful,
You will never measure up to anything
You are never loved
Go back... turn back... why bother
You are not good enough…

Don't give in to your negative voice
Don't let it take control...
Continue to have faith
Faith is believing in what you don't see
Continue to walk forward...
If things are really bad
Take a rest...
But don't turn back...
Keep walking forward...
You are this close to walking out
Walking out of the dark tunnel
Where you have been for many days,
Sometimes may be months or years...
Our creator can see how far you have walked forward...
For he has a bird's eye view...
Not you or me...
So have faith and continue to walk forward...
When things get tough
It's not the time to turn back...

Don't turn back - it's not the time...

Are you looking for Happiness?

So you want to be happy?
Looking for happiness?
Most of us do...
But do you know what happiness means to you?
What does happiness really mean to you?
Have you thought about this?
Not to your parents, not to your family
Not to the world...
But to you?
Do you have an idea...
What makes your heart glow...
Okay most people say that they would
be happy if they win the lottery...
But what are the real chances of that...
Many and many depart without
ever winning the lottery...
So what if you never win the lottery…
Think... think... think... what will make you happy?
Sometimes, they are the little things…
Not necessary big things...
Things that you cant find around you…
Talking to a close friend...
Having a giggle

Or a belly laugh...
Being silly... yes... really silly…
Reading a book
Going out for a coffee with your best friend...
Listening to your favourite music
Going for a walk...perhaps walking
with your bare feet...
Making a garland from wild flowers
Chasing butterflies...
Eating vanilla ice-cream – huum, make a double scoop
These are simple joys in life...
That will make your heart sing
Bring a simile to your face
Dance to your own tune...
Who cares what people might think…
Skip when you walk...
Know what makes YOU... happy...
Then do some every single day...
Make it a priority to be happy
Make a commitment
Find your happiness
And start living it today…

What does happiness really mean to you?

Soul Searching

Do you know YOU?
Huum... you would wonder what sort of question is this
Don't I know me?

Yes, I ask you again – Do you know YOU?
The real you?
Huum... you might think... I am living and breathing...
I am paying bills, and taking care of my children
I am this and that... holding a job, I cook and clean...
How real can I be...

I ask again... Do your know your real SELF?
Do you know your spirit?
Okay now I don't mean that haunted type of spirit
Do you know your soul?
Which is your real self?
The very core of YOU
The gem inside of you
Your truest self? Your sparkling self?
The one that will truly make you happy

Okay it's possible your soul is
buried with so much junk
It is mental junk you have collected from past...

You have no place to dump... so
you dump it on yourself
Days, weeks, months and years go by...
Soon you have buried your soul...
You no longer can find your soul...
You are missing something...
So you look outside...
For him, for her...
For stuff, yes, all kinds of stuff
Your mind tells you... go get this...
You run... then it says... oh..no.. try this..
You run again... then it says... huuum... may be not...
Oh... may be you should try this…
Here you go again... run... run...
left, right, forward and backward...
Like a little puppy dog...
And which ever direction you run
You can't find it...
So now you are sitting... and thinking
I have done everything, looked everywhere
My credit cards are all maxed
My house is full of stuff
But still something is missing
I got married, or I got divorced
I even had children

I finished my degree... and got another one
I thought a masters would help
I got a house... it has a back yard pool
Oh... I even re-did the deck
I got the office I wanted... got a great view
I am looking outside...
But yet it feels empty...
Something is missing...

STOP
Breath…
Be nice to your self…
Look within…
Deep…clean your internal self...
Do what you must do...
It might take some time...
Depending on how much trash you
have dumped on yourself...
Find your inner self...
Some may call this your higher power...
Some godly self...
Some soul or spirit...
Find it... take it out...
Clean it and polish it...
Let your life reflect your soul

Let your mind and body be in sync
with your beautiful soul
The your truest self
Your most authentic self
Bit by bit you will notice...
That what you were really missing
Was your OWN SOUL
And nothing else...

Happy soul searching folks...

Don't Cry.....

Don't cry when I am gone
But smile with me now while I am here
Don't fill my coffin with roses when I am gone
Remember... I can't see them nor smell them...
So what's the point…
But help me fill my life with joy when I am here
I don't need long speeches of how great I have being
When I can't hear anymore
Who are you trying to please?
Me?????
Hello...I am not there... I am gone...
Instead...tell me now – what is in your heart…
Especially the good things you have to say about me
I hope there is at least a few...
Don't feel guilty that you could not
do much when I am gone
Do something with me while you can...
Don't mourn when I am gone
I don't want to have any regrets... I plan not to...
So… Laugh with me now...be with me now...
Help me live my best life now... and
let me help you live yours too...

I don't care whether you attend my funeral
For I am not there to take attendance
I would not know whether you were really there…
Actually there wont be one as I plan
to give my body to the college
So they could make use of me to the fullest...
My skin, bones and teeth and tissues...
Let them learn something and try something new
For the benefit of others…
And let me help them with my dead
body before it turns to ash…

Don't take time off your busy
schedule to attend the funeral
Dont cancel those appointments or keep
those living beings waiting...
I can't see, I can't hear... for I am gone...
Who is there – I am not there – I have departed…
But if you, can take time now
And spend it with me while I am here
I would know that you were there for
me when I needed you most...
Don't spend you hard earn money
to gather merit for me

I know my responsibilities and it's my primary
responsibility to gather merit for myself - I
dont expect you to do this for me...
I have made my path and I am walking on it…
I know I will be okay....
Don't try to remember the date I depart
For it's not important anymore…
But while I am here let's remember the date I arrived…
Don't be mad if I don't leave much wealth for you
For I intend to spend it with you while I am alive
What ever you want to do for me
Do it now... do it with me…
Hold my hand, give me a hug
Make me laugh and smile
Bring me flowers…if you can
They don't have to be expensive
You know I love wild flowers
Don't give me Diamonds or Gold
Crystal or Porcelain
Antiques or Treasures…
You know, I have no value for them…
Any time you are not sure what to give me
Give me a hug... nice and warm…
Or a smile – sincere and true
I value them more than millions

Sing me a song or walk with me
Or tickle me...
If you are busy it's okay...
But drop me a note and tell me how you are…
What ever is in your heart tell me now
While I can hear and see, touch and feel...

If you think I am always going to be around
Then you are in an illusion
Sorry to burst your bubble
But it is the reality of life
We who are born will die one day too...
When we get the call... we have to go…
When it comes we have to go
May not have time for long farewells…

Don't tell me I am negative because
I am talking about death
I am not depressed nor am I sick
I am not out of my mind…
Don't tell me I am too young and I have lots of time
For I have seen death has no age limits
It happens to all at any given time...
I am not saying this to scare you or make you guilty

I am saying you this because it is the truth
Everything else in life is uncertain
But death my dear friend is certain…
That is a sure guarantee

Life Goes On....

Even when
Things are going wrong in very possible way
But yet,
Life goes on
With the dawn of another new day
Birds singing merrily
Sun shining bright
Life goes on…

Things are going wrong in very possible way
Unpaid bills
Jobs lost
Contracts broken
Marriages destroyed
Lives lost
Sicknesses arising
Children crying
Loved ones not talking
friendships lost
Dirty dishes in the sink
Laundry not folded
Problems not solved
Hurtful memories
Broken hearts

Confused minds
Tears still not wiped
But life goes on…
Everything is a mess
Life is a disaster
Can't handle it anymore
Too much on our plate
No more strength to face
Another new day
Don't know what to do
Wish the world would stop
With us…
And wait for us…
And say it's okay… take your time...
Wish it would give us time…
To heal a broken heart
Or
To find a solution
Or to gather enough strength
But it won't stop…
Here comes another day

The world doesn't stop revolving even for a second
The sun does not stop from appearing
The night becomes day

Flowers bloom
Birds sing
Life goes on…
No matter what…
Life goes on…
Life goes on...
Life goes on…

And
No matter what
We are supposed to go with it…

No matter what, life goes on... do you realize this?

Who are you GOD?

Who are you God?
What is your name?
You said to me...
"It does not matter my dear child....
My name does not matter
What matters is you know me...
Dont you?

Some call me this...
And some call me that...
It does not matter
For I am ONE...

I am not here to separate
I am here to unite
I am not here to fight
I am here for peace
I am not here to destruct
I am here to construct
I am not here to demolish
I am here to build and re-build
I am not here to create anger, hate or misery
I am here to spread love, peace and joy

Those who understand this
Know me my child…

It's not about my name
It's not about my colour
It's about what I stand for...

Who is god?
To me it's sense of presence
A powerful and strong presence
I have felt and can not express
Since I was a very young child
Sometimes inside of me
Sometimes around me
And sometimes above me

Where does he live?
He lives in beauty
He lives in music
He lives in love
He lives in compassion
He lives in peace
He lives in joy
He is the early morning dew drop
He is the in the majestic sun rise

I see him.....

yes, I see him...

I see him in the heart of a joyful person

In the laugher of a toddler

In a soft chuckle of a baby

In the glistening eyes of a loving friend

Inside a blossoming flower

In the deep blue ocean

In the mighty rocks

In green valleys and mountains

In sunshine and twinkling stars

In melodious music

And in the fingertips of an artist

In the moving body of a passionate dancer…

God is my friend, coach and my guide

God is with me all night and day

He is one person who has never left me

Strangely I met him

When I lost everything and every one

When I thought I have nothing

And every one has left

But he was there

"shhh... my child.. I am here with you,
I have not left you and I will not leave you…
I am your creator…and you are in my care…
you are here because I need you"

Who is God to you?

Have you heard GOD? A dedication to My Beloved - Boo

Just when I thought...
That everyone has forgotten me
And left me in the dark
Inside this tunnel of scary life
God peeps into my heart
Like a ray of sunshine...
And whispers
I am still here... I haven't left

Just when I thought
I couldn't continue anymore
And I have given all what I have
And nothing more to give
God whispers in my ears
And gently reminds me
No you are not done yet my dear...
You have more to live for
More to give and more to get
More to learn and more to grow

Just when I thought
All my dear friends have forgotten me
And have no use of me anymore...

Here comes God again
And whispers
Did you forget I am your Best Friend?
And I am still here

Have you heard God?
You may call it different names…
You higher power, your inner voice,
your godly self or your divine self
Your authentic self or your inner self...
Jesus, Buddha, Allah, Krishna, Shiv or any other name
This is not about a religion
It's about Your Source
Your Source – Your Creator
And your higher self
That part that reflects your godly self...
Have you found the god in you or
within you or above you?
I hope you have…
If not I hope you invest some time
To find it...
Because it is the greatest gift you can give yourself…
The best ever friend you can find for yourself...

For me - God is
One person who has not disappointed me
One person who has always been there for me
One person who has never isolated me
One person who has not betrayed me
One person who has not disrespected me
One person who has not ignored me
One person who has loved me for who I am
One person who has delivered on time all his promises
One person who didn't forget me
One person who has held my hand
and showed me the way
And I am here to say – its in you too...
It's not just for me but for you too…
Its grace is also for you
Let me remind you again,
It has nothing to do with a religion
or a particular faith group
It's in all of us...
Depending on your belief
It's with you, in you, within you or above you
But it's there for you

So today, take time to find your Source…

Thank You, Thank You, Thank You . . .
Thank you for your love, care, support,
understanding, encouragement and prayers
Thank you for the warm hugs, laughter,
good food and silly jokes
Thank you for accepting me for
who I am with all my flaws
Thank you for being there for me during
the darkest times of my life and checking
up on me every now and then ... It is much
appreciated with lots of gratitude
You all are the precious Jewels of my Treasure
Box - My emeralds, rubies and diamonds

Catherine McEwen
Shiv Sellamuttu, Upendra Cumaranatunga, Alicia
Ali, Kaurobi Banerjee Pandit, Bilkies Bassirullah
Dianne Atay, Michelle Lowe, Ivy King,
Dimple Rana, Bernedette Ferdinand-
Shepherd, Robert Tojza
Dr. Lia Stait-Gardner, Mr. Hamid, Minaz Kaara
Tsering Tsomo, Nicole Sutherland, Sahar Haghjoo
Sonia Nowak, Roshini and Pradeep
Karunatilleke, Bavanthi Ariyaratne
To the team at Balboa Press

To All my wonderful clients of past 20 years – you teach me beautiful lessons every single day!

And special acknowledgement to
Luckey Deva and Neelesh Silva
May you both together do wonderful things
with the beautiful music you create
Unwrap and utilize the gifts that
your Source gave you...

Discover Your TRUE Self and Live
Your BEST Life TODAY!